GO ALL
THE WAY

GO ALL
THE WAY

A Literary Appreciation of Power Pop

Paul Myers and S. W. Lauden

A BARNACLE BOOK | RARE BIRD BOOKS
LOS ANGELES, CALIF.

THIS IS A GENUINE BARNACLE BOOK

Rare Bird Books
453 South Spring Street, Suite 302
Los Angeles, CA 90013
rarebirdbooks.com

For more information, address:
Rare Bird Books Subsidiary Rights Department
453 South Spring Street, Suite 302
Los Angeles, CA 90013

Set in Minion
Printed in the United States

10 9 8 7 6 5 4 3 2 1

Publisher's Cataloging-in-Publication Data

Names: Myers, Paul, 1960–, editor. | Lauden, S. W., editor.
Title: Go all the Way: A Literary Appreciation for Power Pop /
edited by Paul Myers and S. W. Lauden.
Series: The Mixtape Series
Description: Includes bibliographical references. | First Hardcover Edition |
A Genuine Rare Bird Book | New York, NY; Los Angeles, CA:
Rare Bird Books, 2019.
Identifiers: ISBN 9781945572784
Subjects: LCSH Popular music—1961–1970—History and criticism. | Popular
music—1971–1980—History and criticism. | Popular music—1981–1990—
History and criticism. | Popular music—1991–2000—History and criticism. |
Popular music. | Rock music. | BISAC MUSIC / Genres & Styles / Pop Vocal
Classification: LCC ML3470 .G6 2019 | DDC 781.6309/047—dc23

"Power pop at its purest is the music of hit records that miss..."
—Michael Chabon

Contents

Introduction

By Paul Myers and S. W. Lauden

Paul here. For me, explaining the meaning of power pop is a little like explaining what love is. You know it when you feel it, but damn if it's not different for everyone who experiences it. As a songwriter, I've always had a special place in my heart for what I have defined as power pop, and it has always made me feel young and excited, swept up in the euphoric spell of the eternal now, and it's Friday or Saturday night, you just got paid, that girl from school just saw you at the mall, and the limitless potential for adventure is laid out before you like a chiming Rickenbacker guitar. Years ago, Rare Bird asked me to contribute a short story to their literary anthology of prog rock stories, *Yes Is The Answer*, and I wrote a very personal story about my teenage pals and I going record shopping and working out life in the suburbs. After that book turned out so well, I went to Tyson at Rare Bird with an idea, how about a similar anthology, but this time about power pop? Tyson liked the idea and we soon found out that Pulitzer Prize–winning novelist and screenwriter Michael Chabon, my neighbor in Berkeley, California, was as head over heels in love with power pop as I was. We were off to the races, so I put out a back channel, word of mouth search to find other authors, journalists, and musicians who might have a power pop themed essay in them. That took time, too long if you ask me, and I had to put the whole thing on hold for a couple of years while I researched and wrote *One Dumb Guy*, my book about the comedy troupe *Kids In The Hall*. Then, as I was finishing that one, a wonderful thing happened, unbeknownst to me, S. W. Lauden had also approached Tyson with a similar idea, so Tyson put us together to combine our visions for this book. I'll let Steve take it from here…

STEVE HERE. After publishing the Greg Salem punk rock PI trilogy with Rare Bird, Tyson and I were looking for my next project. With dueling backgrounds in music and writing, moving into the world of rock journalism and essays made sense. We were batting ideas around when Tyson mentioned a power pop collection that was on the back burner. I knew it was a perfect fit. I've loved power pop in many of its mutations since I first heard Cheap Trick as a kid, and Paul was the perfect partner in crime. No matter how far my tastes stray into other genres, killer hooks, driving backbeats and strong melodies always suck me back in. I'm thrilled to be part of a collection that brings together so many talented writers and passionate music fans in celebration of power pop.

THIS IS NOT A TEXTBOOK, in some cases the writing isn't strictly journalism so much as personal essays, and shared experiences, so while this book doesn't claim to be the "definitive" anything, we have sincerely tried to bring in as many different takes, experiences, and voices on power pop that we could stitch together before our print deadline closed in, and we think we ended up with a fascinating range of stories. Like a picture, each writer's take on the subject is worth a thousand—actually around two thousand—words, and we think we've taken a pretty cool snapshot here. We close with the immortal words of one of the key architects of the subgenre, the Who's Pete Townshend, who wrote in May of 1967:

> *"Power pop is what we play—what the Small Faces*
> *used to play, and the kind of pop the Beach Boys played*
> *in the days of 'Fun, Fun, Fun,' which I preferred."*

Analog Anthems

By Nancy Rommelmann

A T FIRST THE PHONE is really not yours. You're ten, you don't call anyone; you know your own and maybe your grandmother's phone number by heart.

Then you're eleven, and after your mother goes to sleep, or maybe when she's just not home—it's the mid-seventies and parents are not around much, they're doing group therapy and having affairs—you call 555-1212, which tells you the time: "It is nine-twenty-two and...ten seconds. It is nine-twenty-two and... twenty seconds," and when that gets boring, you switch over to a woman's recorded voice saying what the weather will be in New York City that day and the next. You call her a lot, there's something soothing about it, but it's also about the phone in your hand, a lifeline to the outside, though to what outside you are not quite sure.

By twelve you do sort of know, not in your head so much as in your body, the racing in your chest and the heat between your legs have no place to go, then they do. The Shivvers are singing the exact sensations in "Teen Line," pouring all of it into the telephone, "And it's right, 'cause you called me yesterday, and I had so much to say, and the sun don't have to shine, 'cause my heart's on the teen line." The song is pure pleading and release and makes you feel as though you are being slammed around and running at the same time.

Then you're thirteen, and boys start saying things to you on the street; they say you're pretty, in English, in Spanish. Three boys you've never seen before ask you and your friend for your phone numbers. No one's ever done this, and it seems a reasonable exchange. You hand your number to Junior and Tiger and Roach, and like that they're calling, the phone rings and rings, and your mother asks, Who are these boys? You barely speak into the phone. You're giddy just to hold it, to hear the boys' voices, and then, only Junior's voice, his soft Puerto Rican accent in your ear and, days later, his mouth on yours. You've read, probably in your mother's copy of *The Joy of Sex*, that touching the back of a man's neck makes him...something? Happy? Anyway, you do it, and Junior, who is fifteen, springs up from the bed. "Don't do that," he says, and you think, that was immediate, but it is also the last time you and Junior kiss; he tells you he doesn't trust himself around you, that you are too young.

The phone, which is in the kitchen, rings later in the week. Your mother does not allow phone calls during dinner, and anyway she's had enough of these boys calling, but it's not a boy, it's a girl, and she's screaming something that turns out to be "YAW DAWTAH'S A HAW!" This girl, it seems, has grown up with the boys who have been calling you. She calls again the next night, which is so disturbing to your mother that she gets your father to come over and deal with it, and while it's a little terrifying to hear the girl's voice reverberating through the phone, screaming that you are a whore, you also think, all you did was touch one boy's neck, that you're pretty far from, "For a good time, call..." You have never been in a man's restroom and have no idea if things like this are written on the wall. You know about it only from the

"867-5309/Jenny" song, which you're not sure you like, it's catchy, but it also feels tricky, like a song boys might guffaw at, boys you wouldn't want to hang around with anymore.

You are fourteen, fifteen, and music is changing. You won't know until later that the Ramones and Patti Smith and Blondie are playing over on the Bowery, but you are listening to them, especially *Parallel Lines*, Debbie Harry's Jersey accent full-on in "Hanging on the Telephone," you can see the whole scene, see her in the phone booth, the one across the hall, pleading and flirting and also defiant. You picture her kicking a trash can if she doesn't get her way, and this is how you feel these days.You never go home, the city is yours, you meet other boys, and when Harry sings, "Oh, I can't control myself," it's like she's giving you permission.

Then you are twenty-one. You live in a railroad flat in Brooklyn, and you are lonely for a boy a hundred miles away, a boy who is in your head all the time but you don't call him; you're shy and afraid, but one night you do call. You get his answering machine, which are kind of new things, you're surprised he has one, also, how hearing his voice is like getting warm syrup poured into you. But his voice also makes you feel lonely, to have him at this remove, a voice in a box. The Replacements sing about this, Paul Westerberg sings, "How do you say I miss you, to an answering machine?" He sings, "How do you say I'm lonely, to an answering machine?" You say neither of these things; you leave no message; you hang up and might have called back, to hear his voice again, but *69 has fucked that up.

You are older. Phones change. They have less heroic power. Previously, phones did not belong to you; they belonged to a household, they were on the street; you ducked into phone booths to have an illicit conversation; you could close yourself in one and cry. Now a phone is yours; you hold it in your hand, you play solitary games on it; you take naked pictures of yourself and text them to the man you love. Each time you do, you are thankful the technology did not exist when you were a teenager. You don't believe in the illusion that anything you do with a phone is private, and you miss that about the telephone, plugging in an extra-long cord so you could pull the phone into your bedroom, into the bathroom and close the door, and whisper into it, or simply listen to it ringing on the other end, the hope that someone might pick up like a bubble, like stopping time, an interlude in which to practice what you will say.

"Hello, how are you? Have you been alright, through all those lonely, lonely, lonely, lonely, lonely nights? That's what I'd say. I'd tell you everything, if you pick up that telephone." Jeff Lynne of ELO is singing "Telephone Line," his voice a galaxy away, a satellite signaling for one person only, and the signal is not received. You don't know if you can get through the song, it's crushing you, then the harmonies and emotion sweep you up until you are cradled inside the satellite, Lynne singing, "I'll just sit tight, through shadows of the night, let it ring forevermore," and you are lulled (what choice do you have?) by the belief that as long as the phone is ringing, it might be picked up yet.

It is last month, and you are in Iowa City for a conference. There's an opening party, lots of writers in a bar, and you are drinking a Manhattan. You drink two of them, and then it's midnight, and you don't want any more writer talk, you want to go outside and walk around this new place. You have company. The man you are in love with has given you playlists, for Spotify, you have never had music on your phone and now you do, and take pleasure in it, for the music, sure, and also because it lets you spend time with this man when you are away from him.

You have just put the earbuds in your ears when a girl pitches forward from the bar. She's maybe twenty-two, wearing a skirt the size of an album cover and five-inch ankle breakers on which she cannot walk one step without...whoa! You don't want to scare her, so you gently approach and say, "May I help you get home?" She verily falls into you and says, "Yes, please." You tell her she's going to have to direct you, that you've never been to Iowa City before. "Okay," she says, and off you go, down an alley, up some streets, you have no idea whether Amanda—she's told you her name, and also says, "Sorry, sorry," a lot—is leading you to where she lives, but you're happy this girl is not going to maybe crack open her head on a curb or get caught in a rain that is really starting to come down hard. "Here, here," she says, and you get her up to an apartment building where another student holds open the front door and Amanda disappears inside, no goodbye, and you get the earbuds back in and crank "Starry Eyes" by the Records. You can't believe you missed this when it came out in 1979 and also, how it is making you feel as you did back then, when you listened to "Teen Line," like being grabbed and running at the same time. You hit "replay" and disappear into the lyrics, "I don't want to argue, I ain't gonna budge. Won't you take this number down, before you call up the judge? I don't want to argue, there's nothing to say. Get me out of your starry eyes and be on your way," which you think are about some window-dressing girls getting told they need to scram (but which you later learn is about the band's lazy-ass manager), the narrative hooks you, but what keeps you half-running in the opposite direction of your hotel is the power pop, how hard the band is banging it out, and you are so grateful for this, and while an hour from now you'll be laying your clothes on every available heating vent so you won't be in front of an audience the next morning in half-wet clothes (which you wind up doing nevertheless), right now this song has everything you want; you let yourself get drenched and revolve inside it.

Nancy Rommelmann *is a journalist and author. Her work is featured in the* Wall Street Journal, LA Weekly, The New York Times, Reason, *and other publications. Her most recent book is* To the Bridge: A True Story of Motherhood and Murder, *the story of Amanda Stott-Smith, who in 2009 dropped her two young children from a bridge in Portland, Oregon. She is the author previously of the novel* The Bad Mother; The Queens of Montague Street, *a digital memoir of growing up in Brooklyn Heights in the 1970s; the story collection* Transportation; *and* Destination Gacy, *an ebook about her visit and interview with serial killer John Wayne Gacy. Rommelmann lives in New York City and Portland, Oregon.*

More at nancyromm.com. Follow on Twitter, @nancyromm

On the Road to Power Pop

By Justin Fielding

A S AN INDEPENDENT FILMMAKER with a lifelong love of Beatlesque music, I reached out to several of my favorite power pop artists for help brightening my ornery 2011 slacker comedy, *Inventory*. To my delight, many of the genre's greats agreed to let me place their recordings in the film.

Some years later it occurred to me that, beyond using power pop music on a soundtrack, there should be a documentary that tells the story of this underappreciated subspecies of rock and roll. In 2015, I began traversing the US (and a bit of Canada) to interview dozens of power pop aficionados: musicians, writers, record executives, and promoters. Along the way to making the film (working title: *The Power Pop Movie*), I have interacted with many astute power pop fans on social media and interviewed a few notables among them as well.

Here I'm going to relate major themes I've observed across interviews with approximately 200 subject-area experts: insights, commonalities, and great debates. I began each interview with the foundational question: "What is power pop?"

For musicians, this also connects to the questions of whether they've been called power pop and, if so, how they feel about being so labeled. For all, it was the beginning of a discussion about power pop's history and fortunes.

◆◆◆

FOR THE MOST PART, people define power pop as music that stands on the shoulders of 1960s greats. In particular, music from approximately 1970 on that bears telltale influences from the Beatles (first and foremost), along with the Beach Boys, Byrds, Kinks, and/or Who. A minority opinion is that power pop includes those forefathers themselves, and sometimes even *their* influences, such as Buddy Holly, Chuck Berry, or the Everly Brothers.

This is but one of many matters on which there's considerable divergence among the power pop cognoscenti. Variations on Judge Potter Stewart's "I know it when I see it" (re: defining pornography) are often articulated in trying to nail down precisely what power pop is.

"My idea for Raspberries was to form a band that had the power of the Who, the harmonies of the Beach Boys or the Beatles, and the melodies that were present in all these great songs of the sixties.… No one was doing that, and so my idea was to go completely against the trend."

—Eric Carmen, Raspberries *(The Power Pop Movie* interview*)*

When You Hear It

THE ELEMENTS OF POWER pop most often cited in my interviews include:

- Tunefulness (bright melodies and rich harmonies)
- "Jangle" (such as the ringing tones of twelve-string Rickenbacker guitars)
- Concision (tight songs with instrumentation "played to the song," as opposed to jammy or flashy solos)
- Lyrics that counterpoint happy-sounding music with yearning or melancholy

For some, power pop must—by definition—be powerful. It is typified by "two guitars, bass, and drums" and is often amped up more than in the Beatles' day. However, many of the artists customarily deemed power pop practitioners write and record ballads, include keyboards at times, or otherwise don't fit neatly into the "power" framework. A common answer to this conundrum is that the power can come from the impact of a well-turned song and performance and not necessarily from aggressive playing.

"There's always been a sharp contrast in power pop between the melody and the darkness of the lyrical content."

—Gary Klebe, Shoes *(The Power Pop Movie* interview*)*

What's in a Name?

A NUMBER OF THE interviewees recalled reading the Who's Pete Townshend's coinage of the term "power pop" in a 1967 interview that appeared in *New Musical Express* in England and, stateside, in *Hit Parader*. Scant years after Beatlemania, Townshend decried the fancification of rock music in that Summer of Love era. He likened the Who's single "Pictures of Lily" to the earlier Beatles and Beach Boys sounds, while those bands had moved onto integrating classical and progressive elements and exotic instrumentation layered in via studio magic.

No matter that Townshend was about to embark on the elaborate rock operas *Tommy*, *Lifehouse* (which morphed into *Who's Next*), and *Quadrophenia*. Or that he'd pioneered such forms in his mini rock opera "A Quick One, While He's Away" a few months before.

That aesthetic divide exists in power pop to this day. Some power pop artists keep both feet planted in the early Beatles and Beach Boys ethos, while others are influenced by the whole gamut of their styles, being as inspired by *Sgt. Pepper's Lonely Hearts Club Band* and *Pet Sounds* as much as, if not more than, their formative tunes about dating, dancing, and driving.

It took a decade before Townshend's coinage gained much currency. In 1977, the group Pezband was among the first to use "power pop" in its marketing. Around the same time, the publications *Trouser Press* and *Bomp* began using it to categorize mid-to-late 1970s bands that kept 1960s musical values alive, if somewhat underground, during the heyday of disco and punk.

Artists who were gaining cult, if not bigger, popularity in the power pop boom of the latter half of the 1970s included Dwight Twilley, Shoes, 20/20, and Paul Collins' the Beat. By most accounts, Cheap Trick—now members of the Rock & Roll Hall of Fame—is the most sustainably successful group regularly described as power pop.

As the term became (relatively) established, similarly influenced artists from the earlier part of the decade were retroactively labeled "power pop." These include Badfinger, Raspberries, Big Star, Emitt Rhodes, and *Something/Anything?* era Todd Rundgren.

"It's quite possible that as soon as we were yesterday's news, the very short attention span of the record company executive turned off to the idea of making those other bands the successes that they very well could have or should have been."

—Berton Averre, the Knack (*The Power Pop Movie* interview)

A New Hope

IN 1979, POWER POP reached its commercial zenith. Capitol Records released LA-based band the Knack's single "My Sharona" and album *Get the Knack*, and both topped the charts for weeks on end.

In the wake of this breakthrough for the genre, numerous other power pop bands were signed to major-label deals. Alas, the record industry's enthusiasm for power pop was extremely short-lived.

A powerful reaction against the Knack's meteoric success— termed by some as the "Knacklash"—and the growing commercial acceptance of the hipper, more dance-oriented New Wave and the emerging synth-fueled New Romantic sounds spelled a quick industry retrenchment from the earnest, retro-styled melodicism of power pop.

Artists who were signed when power pop momentarily looked to be the "Next Big Thing" were dropped by their labels almost immediately.

A notable aspect of the Knacklash was that the band was held to account for photographs evocative of famous Beatles poses. This is just one of several backlashes against bands heralded as "the new Beatles."

Years prior to the Knack's emergence, this new-Beatles "curse" could be seen in the fate of Badfinger. Among the first and best-loved power pop bands, Badfinger was, for better and worse, widely seen as "Baby Beatles." Their connections went well beyond stylistic, as they collaborated in numerous ways with Beatles members, and their first releases were on the Beatles' own Apple Records.

It was of course flattering to be considered a protégé of, and even heir apparent to, the most adored rock band in history. But it was also a shadow from which it was near impossible to emerge intact. Badfinger wrote and recorded some of the most indelible power pop hits—songs that could have more than held their own on a Beatles album. But most any power pop fan will avow they didn't receive the commercial and critical rewards that their extraordinary talents warranted.

Badfinger's story took incredibly calamitous turns with two members taking their own lives. The tragic dimension of the effervescent-sounding genre of power pop has affected all too many of its artists, a topic covered perceptively and poignantly in Michael Chabon's *Tragic Magic* essay, which appears in this volume.

Even where the outcomes haven't been quite as devastating, power pop has been a challenging road for most of its practitioners. And for every Badfinger or Raspberries who garnered a handful of hits, there are dozens of worthy power pop bands that never cracked the charts, especially as the 1970s gave way to the 1980s and beyond.

In the years since, previously established and new artists have produced power pop music. The genre seemed to be getting a new lease in the early 1990s with glistening records by Matthew Sweet, Jellyfish, and the Posies, and small labels like Not Lame issued scads of power pop gems in the CD era. But grunge and other sounds won the day, and power pop again fell short of becoming a household name.

Every so often a hit that smacks of power pop, like Fountains of Wayne's "Stacy's Mom," does break through. All along, power pop musicians toil away at making radio-friendly records…but radio has rarely reciprocated.

All this leads to the central mysteries of power pop:

- How did the musical values that were so beloved and successful for the Beatles et al. fall out of fashion? What's not to like about shimmering songs with beautiful melodies and harmonies?
- Why, in the face of continued commercial failure and cultural disregard, do artists continue to create power pop music? *The Power Pop Movie* explores these questions in depth.

"When you get compared to the Beatles, that's the kiss of death. Because if you're not as big as the Beatles, you must not be any good."

—Bun E. Carlos, Cheap Trick (*The Power Pop Movie* interview)

Power Pop, Moi?

MUSIC-INDUSTRY PEOPLE, MANY OF whom personally love power pop, have termed the appellation a "kiss of death." To them it confers negatives that outweigh the positive associations with the charms of 1960s-style pop and with a handful of ear-tickling hits from the genre itself. Among the reasons some artists and labels hesitate to apply the term:

- **Association with catchy music that doesn't catch on with the public.** In fact, when power pop-oriented or power pop-adjacent artists gain marketplace success, by convention, they cease to be called power pop or perhaps commercially benefited by never being so categorized. See Tom Petty (Americana), REM (alternative), Oasis (Britpop), and several popular artists from the late 1970s who were marketed as New Wave or punk but could well have been classified as power pop.

- **Lack of edgy, macho cred.** Some conflate power pop with cloying bubblegum music. And somehow following in the footsteps of the Beatles and the Beach Boys lacks the venerability of, say, following in the footsteps of Robert Johnson, Patsy Cline, Bob Dylan, or the Velvet Underground. A genre propagated by studying hook-laden records via headphones doesn't have the cachet of those whose backstories are honky-tonk roadhouses and hipster dives.

- **Lack of recognition and infrastructure.** Other specialty genres like blues and folk have clubs, record-store sections, and radio shows that cater to their fans, and even non-fans likely have some awareness of those genres' existence. I've heard it said that the only people who have heard of power pop are the fans of power pop.

◆◆◆

THE ARTISTS I'VE INTERVIEWED are all across the spectrum on how they feel about being categorized as power pop. Some wear it proudly, some are ambivalent, and some would rather not be tagged with the label. Many of the first two stripes credit a small but loyal base of fans that reliably supports their new recordings and live performances.

Some avow that it's limiting to an artist to be pigeonholed by any label. But the fact remains that being labeled as, say, a country, jazz, or heavy metal artist bestows financial and reputational benefits that largely don't accrue to power pop musicians, and thus it's more likely to be a hand-wringing decision whether to embrace power pop as a musical identity.

Take a Sad Song and Make It Better

THOUGH POWER POP ITSELF has largely been a commercial also-ran, many power pop musicians have had quite successful careers. After writing and recording a few hits with power pop exemplars Raspberries, Eric Carmen went on to Platinum-level sales as a singer-songwriter. With their ears attuned to the virtues of classic pop playing and recording, power pop musicians are prized band mates, producers, and engineers for artists in more mainstream genres.

Also, power pop music punches way above its weight for song placements in movies, TV shows, and commercials. Freed of the need to be on trend, a power pop song slotted into visual media cuts through to an audience like perhaps no other style.

It conveys exuberance, romance, or melancholy in a superbly listenable form.

For example, in the climactic scene of what may be TV's most-admired show ever, *Breaking Bad,* the song that owns the moment is Badfinger's "Baby Blue." Decades after its release, it then zoomed to the top of the download charts. More recently, the band's power pop classic "No Matter What" was featured in a national ad campaign for Comcast's Xfinity cable service. Raspberries' "Go All The Way" was showcased in the feature film *Guardians of the Galaxy.* And the title songs from shows like *Friends* and *How I Met Your Mother* would be aptly described as power pop, as would many songs featured in popular cartoons like *SpongeBob SquarePants.*

In this new world, where streaming and downloads rule— and where song placement in commercials is considered a legitimate gateway to popularity—several interviewees imagined how 1970s-era power pop would have benefited from today's online tools that enable a specialized audience to find and acquire content directly from artists.

All By Myself

POWER POP MUSICIANS WERE some of the earliest adopters of the DIY music-making culture that is prevalent in the twenty-first century. Inspired by the carefully crafted records coming out of Abbey Road and Gold Star Studios and enabled by increasingly affordable "sound on sound" recording equipment, many power pop artists were among the first to make "one man band" recordings. At the dawn of the 1970s, as Paul McCartney was recording his solo debut at home in London, Emitt Rhodes was doing the same in Hawthorne, California—and many power pop fans would say the latter's self-titled album was even better.

Throughout the 1970s, artists like Tom Marolda (the Toms) and Shoes created power pop masterpieces via home recording, while others availed themselves of bartered or inexpensive studio time garnered from their work at such establishments.

Who Are You?

ONE OF THE MOST consistent observations in talking with so many power pop musicians and fans is that they are an extraordinarily intelligent, articulate, and passionate lot. It takes a bit of a nerd, geek, or whatever affectionate/derisive term one chooses to describe those who avidly pursue a certain spark outside the mainstream.

Given that the seeds of power pop spread mostly by radio and records, its roots are less geographically based than other genres. That said, there are some hotspots worth noting.

The British Invasion (the Beatles and their UK peers and acolytes taking the US by storm in 1963 and soon after) was steeped in American R&B and "girl group" influences. Power pop is largely a US response to the British Invasion (with their aforementioned American contemporaries, the Beach Boys and Byrds, also notable tributaries). There are, though, a few UK-based bands commonly called power pop, as well as some in Sweden, Spain, Australia, and other countries.

In America, the Midwest (home of Cheap Trick, Raspberries, Shoes, and many more) and Los Angeles (home of the Poptopia and International Pop Overthrow festivals) are among the richest veins of power pop. But significant power pop bands can and do emerge from any corner of the US and elsewhere.

The demographics of power pop artists and fans tend toward the white and male, but that's by no means an absolute. I have been somewhat surprised by how many aren't Baby Boomers who grew up listening to each new Beatles release as it came out. Rather, a great many came of age just after the Beatles broke up, and their whole career was available for exploration via parents' or siblings' collections…but before it became trendy for a time to consider the Beatles passé.

One of the happiest findings in this journey has been the new blood that is keeping power pop alive and growing. A side effect of the new modes of music listening is that young people can readily explore, from their phones, whole discographies that once would have required years of record-store spelunking. And some of the obscure gems we felt alone in cherishing are now prized by a new generation of vinyl collectors.

Young musicians who self-identify as power pop are modernizing it, as they have decades of new influences to blend into the mix. To them, the commercial fortunes and what was unhip to someone else in the late 1970s is immaterial. It's just gorgeous music that makes them smile and inspires them to create their own.

Justin Fielding *is an independent filmmaker in Milton, Massachusetts, and a former magazine editor and 1970s record-store clerk who has put in 10,000 hours searching for power pop gems like anyone else who believes the British Invasion deserved to be an endless summer. Find out more about* The Power Pop Movie *at www.powerpopmovie.com.*

They Got the Beat:
The Women of Power Pop

By John M. Borack

"I have absolutely no problem with being labeled as power pop; I love that we're considered a part of such a great music community!"

—Debbi Peterson, the Bangles

"I wasn't aware that the Go-Go's were labeled power pop. I don't pay a lot of attention to labels."

—Kathy Valentine, the Go-Go's

"I don't really relate to power pop quite a lot because of the wussy factor."
—Kim Shattuck, the Muffs

THESE THREE COMMENTS NEATLY encapsulate most artists' reactions when their music has been described as power pop: acceptance, ambivalence, and something close to disdain. In this case, the various reactions from the female side are akin to those of their male counterparts; musicians such as Paul Collins continue to embrace the term power pop while Marshall Crenshaw once colorfully dismissed much of the genre as "ultra-white caca."

So while their feelings regarding the music and the associated labels attached to it (both positive and negative) may be similar, the main difference between the sexes when it comes to power pop is this: there are—and always have been—far fewer females plying the trade than males. Exactly why is anybody's guess, but as Debbi Peterson muses, "I suppose it's similar to saying there aren't as many female bands; there should be more!"

Many of the first wave of female power pop acts from the late seventies on took their aural and/or inspirational cues from pioneering female popsters/rockers such as Fanny, Suzi Quatro, Dusty Springfield (1964's propulsive "Stay Awhile" is an underrated gem from Springfield), and even Lesley Gore. (Joan Jett, who would skirt the power pop genre on more than one occasion, faithfully covered Gore's feminist anthem "You Don't Own Me" in the early eighties.) Girl group legends such as Ronnie Spector and Darlene Love were also quite rightfully looked on as heroes, as were the Beatles and other British Invasion combos. Although her band is considered by pundits to be more punk pop than power pop, the Muffs' Kim Shattuck enthuses, "I'm totally into the British Invasion and Merseybeat." This is borne out by the fact that the Muffs borrowed the title of one of their best-known tunes, "Sad Tomorrow," from the lyrics to the Beatles' "There's a Place"; in addition, Shattuck and company have covered the Troggs and Small Faces as one-offs, as well as Paul Collins' power pop standard "Rock 'n' Roll Girl."

Even though there have been far fewer women traversing the power pop route than men, that's not to say there isn't a wealth of female-fronted pop sounds out there, both old and new. Many point to the heyday occurring from the late seventies to around 1980 or so (at approximately the same time of the meteoric rise and spectacular fall from grace of the Knack), although notable acts such as the Bangles, the Primitives, Juliana Hatfield, Katrina and the Waves, and a host of others would follow later. (the Primitives'

1988 single, "Crash," is an explosively jangly jewel, while Katrina and the Waves' "Going Down to Liverpool"—expertly covered by the aforementioned Bangles—and "The Game of Love," both penned by pop master Kimberley Rew, are lesser known tracks that nearly artistically eclipse the band's ubiquitous hit, "Walking on Sunshine." Meanwhile, Hatfield's 2018 release, *Juliana Hatfield Sings Olivia Newton-John*, was a joyous, non-ironic musical love letter to her childhood favorite.)

As far as that first wave of female power poppers, those rising to the top of the list on the indie side include Midwesterners the Shivvers and Nikki and the Corvettes (hailing from Milwaukee and Detroit, respectively). The Shivvers were fronted by Jill Kossoris, whose pleading vocals and heavy-duty songwriting acumen were proudly displayed (years after the fact, sadly) on the 2014 Sing Sing Records vinyl release simply titled *The Shivvers*. This was the Shivvers album that never was, as the band released a lone, now highly collectible single—1980s sublime "Teen Line"—during their lifetime. The dozen tracks on *The Shivvers* were remixed, remastered, and are classically-styled power pop through and through: there's the Who-like power (and "My Generation"-like vocal stutter) of "My Association," the pop perfection of "Please Stand By" and "Hold On," and the stunning "No Reaction," which is described as "Merseybeat-meets-Blondie-on-speed" in the album's liner notes.

Kossoris' power pop roots dated back to her high school days when she won a contest sponsored by a local radio station that led to Raspberries playing a live show at her school. "They were considered very uncool at the time by all my friends, but I knew they were rockin'," she said later. Eric Carmen would later become a Shivvers enthusiast, and the band not only performed Carmen compositions such as "Hey Deanie" and "It Hurts Too Much" at their live shows, but also recorded an unreleased version of his pre-Raspberries, Cyrus Erie B-side, "Get the Message."

Kossoris—who counts Big Star, Flamin' Groovies, Raspberries, and Badfinger among her power pop perennials—offers up one of the most dead-on definitions of the power pop genre I've ever come across: "[It's] powerful in every sense of the term, but not necessarily in volume: it's emotionally powerful, romantically powerful, lyrically powerful, and melodically powerful. The pop side comes from the craftsmanship of the songs; they're generally well-constructed with no wasted space or down time, and every note and word counts toward the whole for maximum impact. The song is king, not the individual musicians—everything is about the song itself."

Nikki and the Corvettes' lone full-length album was released by power pop champion Greg Shaw on his Bomp Records imprint in 1980. Produced—minimally—by former Romantics member Peter James (who also cowrote the dozen tunes in tandem with Corvette), the premise was simple-yet-brilliant: brief, peppy, guitar-filled tunes with Nikki's (real name: Dominique Lorenz) teen-dream vocals up front and a single-minded lyrical thrust, best summed up by one of the song titles: "Boys, Boys, Boys."

"I never really liked being called power pop back then," Corvette says today. "I always considered us 'bubblegum punk': kind of punk, kind of poppy. It took me a long time to appreciate the term power pop. I was looking up power pop bands on Wikipedia [recently] and was surprised to see myself there." She is a power pop purist in her personal tastes, however, counting Shoes, 20/20, the Romantics, Cheap Trick, the Beat/Paul Collins/ the Nerves/Plimsouls, Dwight Twilley, Phil Seymour, and the Records among her favorites. Although many consider *Nikki and the Corvettes* to be a classic power pop platter released on an indie label that helped kickstart the genre, Nikki had other musical aspirations: "We wanted to be the Shangri-Las meets the Ramones."

A short list of other female power pop of the late seventies/ early eighties—or artists with at least one great power pop tune in their repertoire—would have to include Josie Cotton ("He Could Be the One" and the catchy-but-decidedly-non-PC "Johnny, Are You Queer?"), Robin Lane & the Chartbusters, the 'B' Girls ("Fun at the Beach"), the Little Girls ("The Earthquake Song"), and the Catholic Girls ("Boys Can Cry"). Holly & the Italians' *The Right to Be Italian* (1980), produced by soon-to-be-Go-Go's-producer Richard Gottehrer, was filled with several punchy power pop ditties such as "I Wanna Go Home," "Tell That Girl to Shut Up," and the dramatic "Miles Away." Also in 1980, hitmaking songbird Linda Ronstadt took a power pop turn with her *Mad Love* LP, which featured three compositions each from Elvis Costello and Mark Goldenberg, leader of early eighties power pop combo the Cretones.

While hitmaking machines such as Blondie, the Go-Go's, and the Bangles found commercial gold in a variety of genres— Blondie with dance floor classics such as "Heart of Glass" and "Call Me," and the Bangles with the vaguely annoying novelty chart-topper "Walk Like an Egyptian"—a cursory glance at each band's discography shows a preponderance of power pop.

Blondie's most commercially successful power pop number was the chunky "One Way or Another" (from 1978's *Parallel Lines*), which climbed to number twenty-four on *Billboard* when released as a single; other tracks from the album that fall under the power pop umbrella include "Pretty Baby," "Picture This," the simply wonderful "Sunday Girl," a slightly frenetic take of Buddy Holly's "I'm Gonna Love You Too," and two ace cuts penned by the Nerves' Jack Lee: "Will Anything Happen?" and "Hanging on the Telephone." The previous year found the band scaling power pop heights with their cute update of Randy & the Rainbows' "Denis" and bassist Gary Valentine's winning "(I'm Always Touched by Your) Presence Dear." On the latter tune, and on later efforts such as 1979's "Dreaming," a good portion of the power in Blondie's pop was provided by the superbly creative drumming of Clem Burke.

The Go-Go's discography might be less extensive (just three albums during their initial incarnation), but there is no shortage of catchy, hook-filled goodness throughout. Whether it should all be considered power pop is debatable; bassist Kathy Valentine opines, "I don't know where the line exists between a rock band that writes and records a melodic, jangly, hooky song and a band that someone would call power pop." Still, songs such as Valentine's "We Don't Get Along" (also recorded by power pop semi-legend Phil Seymour on his solo debut), "Yes or No," "Turn to You," and "How Much More" (among others) definitely qualify.

Whereas Blondie rose from the somewhat artsy NYC scene and the Go-Go's began their musical journey in the throes of punk, the Bangles have been purely pop-oriented from the get-go. Their albums contain lovely, harmony-filled covers of songs from power pop titans such as Emitt Rhodes, Kimberley Rew, Alex Chilton, Jules Shear, and Todd Rundgren, while Susanna Hoffs' *Under the Covers* albums with Matthew Sweet found the duo updating tunes from the likes of Chilton, Rundgren, Badfinger, the Bongos, and Marshall Crenshaw. Of course, plenty of the Bangles' originals are dipped in pop magic as well, from the bitter-yet-melodic romantic musings of "James" and "Hero Takes a Fall" to lesser-known gems such as "Complicated Girl" and the Buddy Holly-esque "Crash and Burn" (cowritten by Vicki

Peterson and Rachel Sweet), both from 1988's *Everything*. Unlike musicians who shun the term "power pop," the Bangles' Debbi Peterson continues to embrace the genre: "Most of the music I listen to would be classified as power pop," she says. "The style is so instantly satisfying and addictive, and it means many things to me: happiness, instant gratification, emotion, and power."

John M. Borack *is a California-based music journalist who currently serves as a contributing editor at* Goldmine Magazine, *a monthly music collectors' periodical. Borack is also the author of three books: 2008's* Shake Some Action: The Ultimate Power Pop Guide, *2010's* John Lennon: Life Is What Happens, *and 2018's* Shake Some Action 2.0: A Guide to the 200 Greatest Power Pop Albums 1970–2017. *His next book,* The Beatles: 100 Pivotal Moments that Shaped a Band and its Music, *is scheduled for publication in the near future.*

Putting the Pow! in Power Pop

By Ira Elliot

TRYING TO GET A handle on power pop is not as easy as one might think. For all the usual suspects like Badfinger and Raspberries, Matthew Sweet and Fountains of Wayne, there are dozens of lesser-known bands approaching the genre in myriad ways. Dreamy and psychedelic like the Posies, fast and furious like the Dickies, even big artists that we don't generally think of as power pop occasionally dabble in the genre. Billy Joel's "All for Leyna," Springsteen's "Radio Nowhere," the Clash's "Safe European Home," and Queen's "Need Your Loving Tonight" fit easily under the big, polka-dot power pop tent.

But despite surface differences, all of these four-minute tales of love and loss, yearning and frustration, togetherness and loneliness, do share a few structural similarities. Underlying the catchy melodies, chiming guitars and thumping basses lay the more obscure and mythical domain (Valhalla? Camelot? Bayonne?) of power pop drummers.

It's safe to say that any power pop drummer has two primary sources of inspiration: Ringo Starr and Keith Moon. They are the yin and yang of power pop drumming—Starr representing the more calm, structured, adult approach; Moon the wild, rebellious, teenage id.

You can hear this dynamic in the playing of one of power pop's earliest and most revered drummers, Big Star's Jody Stephens. His drumming on songs like "September Gurls," "Feel," and "O My Soul" encapsulates the combination of solid timekeeping and loose, manic fills.

"At times I'm aware of my influences when I play drums. I'll deliberately think, 'I wonder what Ringo would have done here?' Or I think, 'What would Keith Moon have done here?' But sometimes it's not a thought as much as an impulse. Then it just sort of happens. It's still derived from an influence, but it's however that influence is instilled in you and how it comes out emotionally," Stephens said by phone from Ardent Studios in Memphis, Tennessee.

"Coming up, when we all got together, I don't think I'd heard the expression 'power pop'... It seems like the term 'power pop' came along afterwards. We were just doing what we felt like doing," he added.

The Shining Starr and the Raging Moon

RINGO STARR IS CLEARLY and quintessentially power pop. A steady, hard-hitting rock and roll drummer powering a catalog loaded with guitar-driven, melodic pop gems, his stylistic influence on all rock drummers is deep and across the board. From the fanned hi-hats of "All My Loving" and the cracking snare of "Paperback Writer," to the thumpy toms of "A Day in the Life" and the punchy bass drum of "Revolution." These stylistic elements are central to power pop drumming.

I asked Ben Lecourt, who has collaborated with Emitt Rhodes and plays with Denny Laine of Wings and Joey Molland of Badfinger, to weigh in.

"Ringo is still the model, blue print for the perfect crafted part that will 'wrap' the song like a tailor would design the perfect jacket. What he's done remains the best pop drumming lesson to this day," he said.

And then we have Keith Moon, whose first love was surf groups like the Surfaris, Ronny and the Daytonas, and Jan and Dean. He's probably best known for playing a lot of rapid-fire fills, those dynamic, aggressive flourishes that all drummers enjoy trying on for size...although most end up having to dial it back for fear of overplaying.

Watch live performances of the Who, however, and you'll notice that Moon was acutely aware of the lead vocals, often singing along with Roger Daltrey. So what at first might appear to be arbitrary overplaying turns out to be a running commentary on the lyric. This is the reason his flashiness never takes away from what's being sung, which is an important point.

Beyond the obvious stylistic differences between Starr and Moon, we see two players whose primary concern is for the song. Their focus on how best to frame the chords, melody, and words—to motivate and underscore the song's intent—are core tenets that define all the greatest drummers.

"I've never really thought about what makes a good power pop drum track. I just think about what's going to make a good drum track for this song. It depends on how the singer is delivering it because I listen a lot to the singer, and I listen a lot to the guitar player. I get more energy out of guitar players and singers, but it's always nice to try and lock into what the bass player's doing too," Stephens said.

◆◆◆

AT THIRTEEN, HAVING JUST started to become a serious, teenage rock drummer myself, I spent most of my free time playing along with the radio or albums. By twenty-three, I theorized that you could learn everything you needed to know about this craft by listening only to Starr, Moon, Charlie Watts of the Rolling Stones, and John Bonham of Led Zeppelin—what I called "The Four Horsemen of Rock Drumming." I'll stand by that statement today, some thirty years on.

But we're specifically talking about power pop here, a genre that really didn't start to take shape until a few years into the seventies. So if we look at the drummers of that period more closely aligned with the poppy, snappy Starr and Moon—and less so the bluesy, funky Charlie and Bonzo—my "Four Horsemen of Power Pop Drumming" would likely be Cheap Trick's Bun E. Carlos, Clem Burke of Blondie, Jimmy Marinos of the Romantics, and Bruce Gary of the Knack. (It's interesting to note that my self-proclaimed Horsemen of Rock Drumming are all British while my Horsemen of Power Pop are all American. Which is to say it appears that the preponderance of big power pop bands, in some kind of karmic payback for the British Invasion, were American.)

◆◆◆

IN MY MIND, 1979 stands out as the apex of power pop in the mainstream. Tom Petty's *Damn the Torpedoes*; Buzzcocks' *Singles Going Steady*; the Cars' *Candy-O*; XTC's *Drums and Wires*; ELO's *Discovery*; Nick Lowe's *Labour of Lust*; Elvis Costello and the Attractions' *Armed Forces*; Joe Jackson's *Look Sharp!*; *Dawn of the Dickies*; the Records' self-titled debut; Bram Tchaikovsky's *Strange Man, Changed Man*. I was sixteen at the time and to me it felt like a year-long power pop orgy.

A number of factors were in play here—the rise of New Wave music, the 1977 release of the Beatles' astonishing *Live! at the Star-Club* recordings from 1962, and perhaps a general sense of nostalgia for the sixties that had started earlier in the decade as a fascination with fifties culture and music. I spent the summer of 1979 like just about everybody else hearing *Cheap Trick at Budokan* blast out of the radio night and day.

Cheap Trick's pounding rock was tempered by Bun E. Carlos' loose-wristed style. His left hand often played eighth notes along with his right, ghosting the notes between backbeats like the great Earl Palmer, who is often cited as the architect of rock and roll drumming. (You can hear it very clearly on the opener, "Hello There.") This gave his playing a distinctive kind of old-school lope that was a signature part of Cheap Trick's sound. Bun E.'s galloping tom fills and rock-solid backbeat are the perfect complement to Cheap Trick's Beatlesque songs and a central reason why they became the world's most popular and successful power pop band. "Dream Police," also from 1979, is another fantastic showcase for Bun E.'s Starr/Moon expertise.

Clem Burke showed up to the power pop party overdressed and ready to throw down. Coming from the CBGB's punk scene, the members of Blondie were all stylish characters but Clem's love of high-collared shirts, four-button suits, and skinny, knit ties (Starr!) were perfectly matched by his remarkable red sparkle kits (Moon!). "Dreaming" and "Union City Blue" from 1979's *Eat to the Beat* are perfect showcases for his breathtaking machine-gun fills. His background in rudimental drumming, having played in a drum and bugle corps back in Bayonne, New Jersey, allowed him speed and agility around the kit. Clem's notable gift for showmanship is undoubtedly a direct reflection of his undying Keith Moon worship. His powerful style has allowed him to move effortlessly into the drum chair of a long list of other notable bands including the Ramones, Eurythmics, and Dramarama—not to mention the next band in the 1979 power pop canon.

Recorded late in the year, Detroit's Romantics' first album contains the power pop megahit "What I Like About You," which fuses equal parts early Beatles, Yardbirds, Chuck Berry, Standells, and Neil Diamond. It was Jimmy Marinos' drumming—tough and propulsive, verging on hard rock—that helped make the record a pounding, dance floor staple. Sharing Clem Burke's eye-catching penchant for setting his drums and cymbals completely flat, Marinos was also, like Starr, a lefty on a right-handed kit. But unlike Starr, he played open-handed instead of cross-handed, which allowed him a very powerful back beat. Let's also give Jimmy special mention for being the lead singer on this track, another power pop drumming rarity that he shares with Starr.

But more than any of these songs, 1979 was the year of "My Sharona." Certified Gold and hitting number one on the US Billboard charts, "My Sharona" was a power pop juggernaut and when it exploded onto the radio, it was drummer Bruce Gary who lead the charge. The aggressive, flam-filled kick, snare, and tom intro, lifted from Smokey Robinson's 1967 "Going to a Go-Go," was absolutely undeniable.

Bruce was an LA session player who was capable of sounding wildly spontaneous while remaining completely airtight. There's not one misplaced hit on any Knack song, but the performances are never mannered or stiff. Unlike most recordings of late seventies where the drum sound was thumpy and dead, Bruce's drums were bright and ringing, one of the reasons that *Get the Knack* was such a breath of fresh air. The longer, album version of "Sharona," "Let Me Out," and "Number or Your Name" are all textbook examples of how to channel Moon into a contemporary pop song.

In these four power pop drummers, we see both the solid timekeeping skills of Starr and the visceral enthusiasm of Moon. Of course, these four choices are admittedly a bit arbitrary since there are many other great drummers I would love to name-drop here. Topping that list is Jim Bonfanti, the Raspberries' first drummer. His remarkable rolling, tripping tom fills on "Go All the Way," and particularly on "Tonight," are nothing less than power pop scripture. Like Stephens from Big Star, Bonfanti fully inhabited the Starr/Moon nexus.

◆◆◆

I'VE MET QUITE A number of people over the years who feel Ringo somehow doesn't rate because his style is overly simple and devoid of "chops"—those slick, learned phrases that simply show how long a drummer has practiced alone in a room on a slab of hard rubber. To them I say, virtuosity is not a prerequisite.

In my opinion, Ringo had something much more valuable—the confidence of someone who'd spent a lot of time getting rooms full of people to get up and dance. But he wasn't fancy. He was bone simple, and this is what I call "The Tao of Ringo." Part of the beauty of power pop drumming, like all rock drumming, is that it doesn't necessarily require a high degree of technical skill. Rock and roll music is a folk art; you don't need a degree from Berklee to make it.

What you do need is a solid set of basic timekeeping skills, three-limb coordination (which I guesstimate can be developed in about the same amount of dedicated time it would take to be a passable skateboarder, let's say) and, most importantly, musical empathy—an innate connection with and love of music that transcends skill. You simply need to be the right person for the job at hand, which may have as much or more to do with your personality as your ability.

"I think what's key to the essence of power pop drumming is attitude and maintaining a youthful outlook and feel to one's playing," said Dennis Diken, drummer for the Smithereens. I was incredibly fortunate to work as a drum tech for Diken in the nineties and consider him to be one of the best power pop drummers ever.

"One of the greatest compliments I ever received was from John Duckworth, the drummer from Syndicate of Sound whose '66 snotty, jangly, round-the-kit fill-laden 'Little Girl' was a major air drum record for me when I was nine years old. He said, 'Hey, I was watching you play, and I can tell you're a talented drummer but man, you played that set like you were seventeen!' I was forty-three at the time. I'm a few years on now, but I still try to keep that teenage spirit burning whenever I get behind the kit with the Smithereens."

When it comes to power pop, the importance of the drummer's attitude and energy cannot be understated. This is why I believe power pop has been and will continue to be a pursuit for musicians of any age, particularly young ones. Artists are inspired by the things they love, and it's hard to think of a more enduring love affair than the one we have with the Beatles. Young musicians will invariably attempt to write songs that somehow echo their style. Most will try and fail, but even now—this very second—there's a band in a basement or a rehearsal room somewhere writing one of those songs that will send you straight to power pop heaven.

And they're gonna need a good drummer.

Ira Elliot *has been a rock and roll drummer all of his adult life. After graduating the prestigious High School of Performing Arts, he began playing in bands in his native New York City. In 1983, he became the drummer in garage rock revivalists The Fuzztones and in 1995 joined indie rock band Nada Surf with whom he still plays. He is also a founding member of Hamburg-era Beatles band Bambi Kino. He lives happily with his wife, Jen, and daughter, Vivian, in sunny Sarasota, Florida.*

Power Pop as Beatles Obsession

By Jeff Whalen

ON FEBRUARY 13, 1977, the *Providence Journal* in Rhode Island published a story putting forth the idea that the Beatles had secretly reunited and, using the band name Klaatu, recorded a new album. The rumor took off nationally.

There were clues everywhere, in a "Paul is dead" kind of way.

- First, Klaatu was on Capitol, the Beatles' record label in America. So there's that, for sure.
- There are no musician or songwriting credits given on the record and no photos of the band in the record or in any of the promotional material. The band had never played live, given interviews, or made any public appearances of any kind.
- Capitol Records denied knowing what was up with the band. They claimed to have never met, talked to, or seen the members of Klaatu. A Capitol spokesman said that they simply bought two master tapes from a man named Frank Davies, who worked for a different record company in Toronto. Davies told Capitol that the members wanted no publicity—that the music should speak for itself.
- The name "Klaatu" is a reference to the 1951 sci-fi movie *The Day the Earth Stood Still*. The cover of Ringo's *Goodnight*

Vienna album features a photo of Ringo, as the character Klaatu, superimposed onto a scene from the film. (Slash's mom, who was dating David Bowie at the time, designed the suit Ringo is wearing in the photo. Not a clue, probably, just thought I'd mention it.)

- Paul had closed a recent Wings concert in Boston by saying, "I'll see you when the Earth stands still." When Paul's office was contacted about it, they just said it meant, "See you next time."
- The front cover of *Klaatu* features a drawing of a sun that looks kinda like the sun on the inside of George's record, 33⅓.
- Near the end of the Klaatu song "Sub-Rosa Subway" there is a Morse code message that supposedly reveals the true identity of the band members. Dallas radio station KFWD convinced the US Coast Guard to help try to decipher the Morse code, "and is working on voice prints from the vocals," according to an article in the *Daily Texan*. The results were inconclusive. KFWD disc jockey Dan Van Dyke said, "The best that we can determine right now is that one of the members of Badfinger formed the band." (I realize this all sounds like a joke, but it is real, real, real.)
- According to several newspaper reports, a disc jockey in Wisconsin played the record backwards and heard "It's us, it's us, the Beatles" in one of the songs. Who could possibly argue with that?

The Klaatu-is-the-Beatles phenomenon is largely forgotten these days—I only know of it because the Welsh band the Pooh Sticks recorded a Klaatu song instead of a Beatles song for a Beatles covers compilation album—but back in the seventies it was a deal. Most major newspapers covered it. The Klaatu album, which had been released in 1976 to no buzz and even fewer sales, was on its way to the cutout bin when it was rescued by the rumor. As the rumor took off, the album started selling, eventually reaching #32 on the US album charts. The Carpenters covered the opening song from the record, "Calling Occupants of Interplanetary Craft," taking it to #32 on the Billboard Hot 100 that year.

Listening to the record now, one wonders what everyone was smoking in the 1970s, and the answer is probably marijuana with some PCP in it. It's hard to imagine anyone thinking Klaatu might really be the Beatles. Not that the record is bad—though much of it is—it's just that you know it's not the Beatles in the same way you know any clear and apparent thing. The most Beatles-y song is "Sub-Rosa Subway," which is an okay song, but it's unremarkable and obvious in its Beatles moves—French horns, Paul-ish vocals, talking about old-timey stuff, that kind of thing. By far, the best song on the record is "Calling Occupants of Interplanetary Craft," the song the Carpenters covered, which is actually a psychedelic pop triumph and definitely worth a good, loud listen. (Try listening to it after smoking some pot with PCP in it.) It's a fun, genuinely good song, but there's nothing about it that should make anyone think it was literally the Beatles. If there's anything on the Klaatu record that might secretly be a different band, it's "Sir Bodsworth Rugglesby III," which sounds like it could be an unreleased track from *The Muppet Movie* soundtrack, something sung by Rowlf the Dog. It does! Check it out! I'm starting the rumor right now!

After finding out about the Klaatu hoax—oh, it turned out that Klaatu was a band of Canadian studio musicians, by the way. They ended up putting out five albums, each one less good than the one before (maybe M. Night Shyamalan was in the band? Can we start that rumor?), and never lived down the Beatles thing—the first thing I did was track down the record and buy it. Why? Because this is what a certain kind of Beatles fan does.

A certain kind of Beatles fan always wants more, more, more. More! And if you can't get any more actual stuff by the actual Beatles, you find ways to continue it by seeking out bands that keep that Beatles-y feeling going. And if you're a fan with musical dreams of your own, you start your own band and secretly pretend you're in the Beatles. These bands are called power pop bands.

Look, every rock band starts off trying to straight up copy the bands that speak to them. For power pop bands, it's not a case of just looking at pop music generally and taking a bit from here and a bit from there, with the Beatles being just one source of inspiration. *Being in a power pop band is an expression of wanting to be in the Beatles.* You want to be in the Beatles. You want to make 100 percent perfect pop music with your friends and run down the street with a mob of girls chasing you. To be young and funny and artful and stylish and as admired by your peers as by the girls who are still chasing you down the street even though you went into a phone booth and came out wearing fake beards.

This is true of me and of people like me, now, years removed from it. But it must've been super true of music fans during the Klaatu episode. Those people had been alive and around for the Beatles when the Beatles were actually putting out music. The sense of loss of not having the Beatles anymore—and to have to deal with the emotionally thrilling (and draining) possibility that they might get back together and make more records—must've been sharper, more alive.

As Capitol Records publicist Bruce Garfield explained about the Klaatu thing at the time, "People are going crazy over it. The world wants the Beatles back, you know?"

Klaatu is not an according-to-Hoyle power pop band. Most of their Beatles-y elements are drawn from post-1967 Beatles and power pop typically values the pre-1967 stuff. But the frenzy around their album speaks to the unusual intensity of Beatles obsession during the late 1970s and early 1980s—which just happens to be power pop's golden age. And this is my main theory here: as the people who were children when the Beatles first hit America reached their mid-twenties and formed their own bands, power pop flourished, informed by the bands' desire to recreate the Beatles feeling of their youth.

The same thing goes for fans, too. The world owns the Beatles, but during this era, power pop fans got to have their own mini Beatlemania when they liked Cheap Trick or the Knack, or an even mini-er one when they liked the Romantics or the Plimsouls, or an even extra-mini-er one when they liked the Toms or the Records or the Beat or the Pop or Radio City or the Speedies or whoever. When a power pop fan listens to Emitt Rhodes' solo record, they're not really trying to listen to something new and exciting; they're trying to listen to someone—someone who is like they are—working through their Beatles feelings.

Bob Stanley, pop writer and guy who was in some band called Saint Etienne, argues in his super-good *Yeah! Yeah! Yeah! The Story of Pop Music from Bill Haley to Beyoncé* that a pop fan will particularly cherish whatever music was on the charts when he was ten years old. That's around the age when you "fall in love with any guitar, any bass drum, soak up the whole of the Top 20, and love it all without question." Like, if you were ten when "Rave On" by Buddy Holly came out—or "Mr. Roboto" or "Tubthumping" or whatever—then that song is going to enjoy a more magical place in your heart than if it came out at some other time in your life.

Imagine then what it must've been like to see the Beatles on Ed Sullivan at age ten? As my friend said, "*that's* mainlining the hard stuff, baby."

Perhaps we should discuss the Beatles elements that are essential to power pop. Maybe, but don't you think it largely goes without saying? Whatever power pop is—and arguing about its definition is one of the many pleasures of being a power pop fan—most reasonable people can agree that the Beatles, particularly pre-1967 Beatles, provide the working blueprint for the genre. Handclaps? Check! Lively, hooky, three-minute pop songs, mostly focusing on boy-girl stuff? Sure! Four guys? Usually! Everybody dressed pretty much alike, maybe with neckties? Open to it! A two-guy singing-songwriting approach with lots of harmonies? You betcha! Hats? Nope! Mustaches? No way! Drummer sings one song? Why not!

Are the Beatles themselves power pop? No, and for a number of reasons! One being the fact that *nostalgia* for the Beatles is a key propulsive element for the power pop band.

But what about the Who? The Beach Boys? Certainly power pop bands owe a lot to those groups, too, right? Sure! Power pop often employs sounds that aren't particularly Beatles-based, such as bigger guitars and busier drums *a la* the Who, or Beach Boys-y harmonies *a la* the Beach Boys. Check out the Raspberries' masterful use of the Beatles-Who-Beach Boys model in songs like "Go All the Way" and "I Want to Be With You." But the Who and Beach Boys moves are optional; the Beatles connection is essential. If a band emulates the Who or Beach Boys without employing the values that those bands also share with the Beatles, it's not a given that the band would be considered power pop. But if a band tries to make an album that sounds exactly like *Meet the Beatles*, without any Who or Beach Boys, they'd still be power pop.

And you gotta keep it pre-1967. Your Beatles obsession needs to be focused early or mid-career Beatles, and you get out before

Sgt. Pepper's. As the Beatles got more studio-based, they lost some of the straightforward energy and live-band presentation that power pop cherishes. This is why bands and songs that are greatly influenced by late Beatles aren't usually considered power pop. ELO, the Bee Gees, 10cc, etc. "So You Are a Star" by the Hudson Brothers is great, and super Beatles-y in every way—McCartney in the verse, Lennon in the chorus—but it's late Beatles-y, so it's not power pop. And the Hudson Brothers had mustaches and often hats, so no soap. Similarly, though from a non-power pop era, Tears for Fears' undervalued "Sowing the Seeds of Love" is strictly psychedelic Beatles and so not power pop. Also, it's by Tears for Fears, and you can't become a power pop band if you're already established as something else. The Rubettes' "You're the Reason Why" is a good example: total power pop, but by the Rubettes, so no. Also true of established actors who make power pop records: Rick Springfield, David Essex, Drake Bell. Not power pop.

(As an aside, I just want to add that "Sowing the Seeds of Love" is so good you'd think you'd occasionally hear it at the grocery store instead of "Shout," a song I did not realize when I was a kid that I'd have to hear several times a week for my entire life.)

But back to the golden age of power pop. There's always a lot of interest in the Beatles, no matter what era you're talking about, but in the late 1970s and early 1980s there was a marked increase in Beatles nostalgia everywhere. Said the *LA Times* in 1977: "A mild form of Beatlemania, that frenzy of the midsixties, is flaring up again. We have enough distance from their work to be able to examine it from a fresh perspective. Their music has had time to sink in. Most of it hasn't dimmed with age and, in fact, seems solid enough to ultimately be for the second half of the century what the works of George Gershwin and Cole Porter were for the first half."

And as Thomas Kessler, the writer of the Klaatu *Daily Texan* article, noted: "It's been ten years since *Magical Mystery Tour* was released and the world is still spinning records backwards for Beatle messages that may or may not exist. The Beatle obsession is bordering on religion."

Beatles stuff was everywhere at the time. If you got a minute, I can go into it! Got a minute?

- The Beatles charted with "Got to Get You Into My Life," taking it to #7 in 1976. Was it in a movie or something? No! New remix or different version or something? Nope! They just put it out again six years after they broke up and it went to #7.

- The musical *Beatlemania!* opened on Broadway in 1977 and became a big deal. The guy who played John was Marshall Crenshaw, a power popper in his own right. He had a hit in 1982 with "Someday, Someway," a kind of Buddy Holly-informed look at the early Beatles.

- Robert Zemeckis' directorial debut, *I Wanna Hold Your Hand*, was released in 1978. It's a comedy about some New Jersey girls trying to meet the Beatles at their *Ed Sullivan Show* debut. Pretty good!

- "Stars on 45 Medley" was a #1 hit for the Dutch group Stars on 45 in 1981. It was basically a medley of early Beatles songs set to a disco beat, heavy on the claps. It was put together by a dude from Golden Earring, who also wrote the catchy non-Beatles part of the song (*"The Stars on 45 keeps on burning in your mind!"*). The John parts are sung by a guy named Bas Muys, who had been in a very Beatles-y band called Smyle. (Smyle is actually pretty good, by the way, though they're so Beatles-y that they may overshoot the power pop label and go straight into Rutles territory.)

- The bad movie *Sgt. Pepper's Lonely Hearts Club Band* came out in 1978 and was bad. On paper it sounds like it should be at least worth a look—Peter Frampton and the Bee Gees starring in a Beatles-song-based rock and roll fantasy, and Steve Martin's in it, and the music's produced by George Martin—but it is not.

- Not as bad as *Sgt. Pepper's*, but still super bad, was *Birth of the Beatles*, a 1979 TV movie about the Beatles' pre-stardom era in Liverpool and Hamburg. Ever see it? It's boring, and you spend most of the movie trying to figure out which actor is supposed to be which Beatle.

Power pop bands leaned into it. The Knack famously looked all Beatles-on-the-Ed-Sullivan-Show on the back cover of *Get the Knack*. 20/20 and lots of other American bands sang with openly Beatles-y accents. The cover of Utopia's very Beatles-y record *Deface the Music* in 1980 was straight-up *Meet the Beatles*. Some theories have Shoes getting their name from an old Beatles interview in which John and Paul say they could've just as easily been called the Shoes as the Beatles.

One power pop band from New York, the Yardleys, never broke through, though it wasn't due to a lack of pretending they were the Beatles. Unsigned, they traveled to England in 1979 and somehow managed to be the last band to play at whatever version of Liverpool's Cavern Club was then in business before the venue closed permanently. From there, they secured a three-week residency at the Star Club in Hamburg, Germany. Oh, and their UK manager was Brian Epstein's brother, Clive. You can't make any of this stuff up.

Though the Yardleys music is perfectly acceptable power pop, it's likely that one of the reasons they never made a success of things is that their attempt to associate themselves with the

Beatles played to power pop fans as cheesy. Indeed, how you signify your understanding of what makes the Beatles great is of crucial importance in the power pop world.

Remember what John said that one time? "Christianity will go. It will vanish and shrink. I needn't argue about that; I'm right and I'll be proved right. We're more popular than Jesus now. I don't know which will go first—rock and roll or Christianity. Jesus was all right but his disciples were thick and ordinary. It's them twisting it that ruins it for me."

The equating of religion and Beatles obsession in the first part of the quote is certainly apt. A certain kind of Beatles fan spends his life sorting it out until it becomes a kind of religion, a kind of value structure, a kind of companion guide as you live your life. You fellowship with other converts. You debate meanings. You play records backwards. You strive to be like them in life and art. During the "WWJD?" era, I heard more than one rock producer talk about "What Would Beatles Do?" when stuck with a quandary in the studio.

But it's the last couple sentences of John's quote that are relevant in terms of power pop. Lots of thick and ordinary people say they're Beatles fans—"'Imagine' is my favorite Beatles song," they might say, knowingly—in a way that makes a certain kind of Beatles fan feel that everyone on Earth is stupid. How you express your affiliation with the Beatles is important. Being in a power pop band or being a power pop fan is a way of signaling to others what kind of Beatles fan you are. You demonstrate the depth and the coolness of your understanding of the group. Yes, most people like the Beatles, but you like them in a fucking rad way, because the Beatles are fucking rad and so are you.

Jeff Whalen *is a musician and librarian from Long Beach, California. He is the lead singer of the rock band Tsar.*

Tragic Magic

By Michael Chabon

THEY CALLED THEMSELVES BIG Star and never made it big or found stardom, and there, along with a 2:49 song called "September Gurls" that shimmers and chimes with all the hopeless longing you ever felt for someone you never got to hold or to keep, is the pocket history of power pop.

The expression of unfulfilled longing forms the seam along which irony and sincerity meet, or at least come most nearly to resemble one another. Here we find power pop: at the point where the sincere jangle and thump of two guitars, bass, and drums meet those high harmonies and handclaps that have been ironic from the day, sometime in 1966, that the Beatles renounced them. The four-disc *Keep an Eye on the Sky* (Rhino Records, 2009) is, therefore, a perfect power pop artifact. In handsome, heavy-weight cardstock, it manages to enwrap the fervent sincerity of fannish completism with the irony that inheres in any grand monument to something most people have never heard of.

Pete Townshend is generally credited with having invented the term "power pop" to describe the sound of the Who when they were still a singles band: guitar and drums pushed up front, the drums big and chunky, the guitars at once hard-edged and melodic and fulfilling the Chuck Berry injunction to ring like a bell. Sharp harmonies, tight song structure complete with bridge, and in the lyrics, an oblique, even backhanded approach to the sentiments and desires conventionally expressed in a three-minute hit record.

Power pop in its essential form, however, did not come into existence for a number of years after it was first identified. Like so much of the greatest work turned out by popular artists of the 1970s, true power pop is quintessential second-generation stuff, self-conscious art in which the construction of catalogs and hierarchies beloved by fandom are fully matched by its dizzy passion. Every work of popular art is a cursor on a ruled scale of influences and sequels, but in the best second-generation work, all the pleasure is in the sliding. When in the first half of the decade, the Raspberries, Badfinger, and Big Star (along with the Todd Rundgren of "Couldn't I Just Tell You" and "I Saw the Light") invented the sound that came to be known as power pop, they were not revivalists. They looked backward to the music they had come of age loving—the astonishing run of perfect singles produced by British and American beat bands of the mid-sixties—but they did not attempt to play it so much as allow it, in the most acutely nerdish sense of the term, to inform the songs they wrote.

The second salient feature of power pop, along with its avowed status as a kind of fandom, is that it is happy music—eminently "poppy"—which depends for its power on the cryptic presence, in a lyric or a chord change or a bit of upside-down vocal harmony, of sadness, yearning, even despair. This strand of pop darkness can be found right off the bat, in the founding documents of the genre, like the Who's "Pictures of Lily," in whose final stanza the song's narrator discovers that his pinup dream girl has "been dead since 1929," or the Beach Boys' "Wouldn't It

Be Nice," where the sadness and yearning are smuggled into the melody, the harmonies, the lyrics, and even the title, which marks the broken place, the gap between the wish and the world. True power pop is rueful and celebratory at the same time, glorifying desire and frustration, which is why so many power pop songs concern themselves with the subject of Tonight, or Tomorrow Night, or Saturday Night, or some other night that will only be perfect for as long as it can be deferred. Depression stalks the genre, from Brian Wilson and Emitt Rhodes to the dual suicides of Badfinger, Pete Ham and Tom Evans; from Big Star's Chris Bell, who struggled with profound depression right up to the night in 1978 that he crashed his Triumph TR-6 into a telephone pole; to Material Issue's Jim Ellison; and to Doug Hopkins, the lead singer of the Gin Blossoms. All the clouds of power pop are worn inside out to show the silver lining.

Finally, power pop at its purest is the music of hit records that miss. Pick up any of Not Lame's *International Pop Overthrow* collections or the numerous sets that Rhino has issued over the years—*Shake Some Action* and *Come Out and Play*, or the three volumes of *Poptopia*—and you will find that from about 1970, when Badfinger released the first true power pop record, "No Matter What" (which admittedly went to #8 on the US chart), an astonishing amount of effort and genius and chops have been expended by the practitioners of power pop to create a large number of equally well-crafted, tightly played, buoyant-yet-wrenching surefire hit songs that went nowhere, moved no units, never made it out of the band's hometown, or came heartbreakingly close to Hugeness before sinking, like the Records' "Starry Eyes" or Bram Tchaikovsky's "Girl of My Dreams," back into the obscurity that is the characteristic fate of all great power pop. Something—maybe it's the self-consciousness, or the darkness, or that handclap of irony—dooms the would-be hit songs of power pop, so that the Raspberries' wonderful, parenthetically telling "Overnight Sensation (Hit Record)," with its backup singers hopefully, achingly praying "mumber one!" over and over in its chorus, never rose any higher than mumber eighteen.

But Badfinger and the Raspberries managed to land seven songs apiece in the US weekly Top 100. Of the three founding bands of the genre, only Big Star—whose first album was entitled, with classically power pop ironic sincerity, *#1 Record*—attained the kind of spectacular failure that forms the paradoxical basis for true power-pop greatness. And yet they are now, to date, the only band among the three to earn the kind of fannish apotheosis that a box set like *Keep an Eye on the Sky* represents. The set collects all the tracks from the three canonical albums— the 1972 debut, 1974's *Radio City* (which contained "September Gurls," the greatest number-one song that never charted), and the glorious, ragged, haunted, sweet, brutal third album, 1992's *Third/Sister Lovers*, which went unreleased for years after it was originally shelved due to utter lack of commercial interest and which is at once the band's best album and barely power pop at all. *Keep an Eye on the Sky* also rifles the vaults of Ardent Studios to find alternate mixes and demos for many of the songs from those records, while offering a brief but instructive sample of the work done by Chris Bell and Alex Chilton (guitars) immediately before they teamed up with Andy Hummel (bass) and Jody Stephens (drums) to form Big Star, naming themselves after a local Memphis supermarket chain. The A and B sides of Chris Bell's only post–Big Star solo release are here, too, including the remarkably sad power pop anthem "I Am the Cosmos," which zooms out the yearning of power pop by powers of ten all the way to the edge of creation and then zooms it right back in again to the singer, a tiny speck of loneliness on a gorgeous sea of guitars.

Disc four is taken up with an unearthed live recording of the band, sounding bright and fiery and well rehearsed, playing sometime in early 1973 at a place called Lafayette's Music Room in Memphis, Tennessee, before what has to be accounted the least-interested audience—they were waiting for Archie Bell and the Drells to come on—in the history of live performance. Never has the automatic "thank you!" of a frontman at the mic sounded more hollow than in the mouth of Alex Chilton just before he launches into a blistering, celebratory, futile cover of the minor T. Rex hit "Baby Strange."

All the studio material gathered on the first three discs has been heard and can be found in many other places, in one form or another, but those who love Big Star will here find ample reinforcement for their affection, while those who have yet to experience the pleasure of the music will discover exactly what it takes to start a cult, to distinguish oneself from great bands like Badfinger and the Raspberries: a ripeness, perhaps Southern, tinged with soul, that like all ripeness teeters between the sweet and the rancid, as power pop always risks rancidity (the Knack) or flirts dangerously with the saccharine (the Rubinoos). But it's in listening to the fourth disc, capturing live near the peak of its talent one of the best rock bands that America ever produced—three guys (Chris Bell, distraught over the failure of #1 Record, having departed the band) totally in love with the tragic magic of power pop, with the sound of a heart breaking to the accompaniment of handclaps and angelic la-la-las, playing their own jaded hearts out, Chilton singing, on a song like "Watch the Sunrise," with an aching, self-mocking tone of overripe sweetness, and the drums and bass keeping everything steady and well shaped and rock and roll—it's on the fourth disc of *Keep an Eye on the Sky* that the profoundest truth about power pop begins to emerge: those people gathered at Lafayette's that evening in January 1973, waiting to do the *Tighten Up*, simply do not give a shit. They chatter and laugh between songs, banging their plates and glasses. They don't catch the irony; or that is all they hear. They don't see how a pop song, powerful or not, can take a spectacularly ironic sentiment like, say, "I can't get no satisfaction," and turn it into a desperate plea for connection, for a world that makes sense, a world in which no one who doesn't smoke your brand of cigarette could ever be mistaken for a man. Power pop is a prayer offered by atheists to a god who exists but doesn't hear. *Keep an Eye on the Sky* is a worthy temple of this bittersweet faith.

Michael Chabon *lives in Berkeley, California.*

Mr. Earl The Jesus Of Cool

By Allison Anders

It was the jukebox that was the draw. The basement where the bands played was under construction, being brought up to code after the law had shut it down. Maybe that was why Fred Grainger, the guvnor, knew he had to do something to make up for his losses on live entertainment and set about to make that jukebox like no other in the summer of 1973.

We heard about the place from our flat mate Tim Boswood. He walked in after pubs closed around midnight, came up stairs of our house, wearing his old green army jacket. He looked in on us from the doorway to our room, Phil's and mine. Tim's long blonde hair flowing down and a smile through his Viking beard, as he shared a hash joint with us, "I've just found the coolest pub,", Tim said. He'd stumbled upon it quite by chance, cool people, great beer, and this jukebox, oh the jukebox. A big crazy mural. Psychedelic? "No, ridiculous," he said, "funny". Taking the piss out of psychedelia.

A Kentucky-born girl eighteen years old I was fresh in the Mother Country less than month ago from the San Fernando Valley—Van Nuys, California, to be specific. Where the cultural highlight was cruising cars on Wednesday nights. To rescue myself from my brutal SFV boredom, I'd saved up my tips waitressing at a coffee shop after dropping out of high school and had come here to live with an English boy I met on a Greyhound bus in Amarillo, Texas. Phil White from Surrey, of York University where he and Tim had studied philosophy together. And now we all found ourselves sharing a house in Islington, which, despite being posh now, was then regarded as "a rather drab working-class neighborhood of little charm".

The Hope and Anchor was about a seven-minute walk from our flat; just up St. Paul's Road to the roundabout left on Upper Street and there she was in her Victorian glory at Islington Park Road. Our first euphoric evening there was mainly spent proliferating that jukebox crammed with off-singles, not the stuff they necessarily played on the radio, and vintage tracks as well (which is a no brainer now but was not anywhere to be found back then). There was a Kinks single from 1966, "I Need You," with a faded label, alongside "Right Place Wrong Time," by Dr. John, and a Brinsley Schwarz single, "Shining Brightly," that had a *handwritten* label.

I had come to London with virtually no money. I don't know what I was thinking or what my mother was thinking to let me board that British Caledonian flight, but one thing was certain now: I needed a job. I had briefly worked as a waitress at a café on Holloway Road—absolutely disastrous. First of all, no one tipped. Secondly, I didn't know bangers and mash from a full English breakfast, and I was constantly delivering the wrong food to the wrong table and yet only once did someone politely complain and he clearly felt so guilty about it he was my one and only tipper.

So I was literally pounding the pavement looking for a job, and saw I was nearing The Hope and Anchor and had a thought, "Oh my god, what if," which then gave way to a prayer, "Please have a job for me," and shocker—there under the Victorian arches and taped on the window to the door a flyer "Help Wanted."

The guvnor Fred Grainger was the face and affable host of The Hope And Anchor but the person who really ran the place was his gorgeous wife, Sue. The pubs closed back then between about 2–5:00 p.m. and it was downtime now. I made myself heard at the door.

Sue came down the stairs and listened to my breathless inquiry about the job advertised and with her arms folded she looked me first up and down and then directly into my eyes. She brought me upstairs to their flat, hers and Fred's where two little kids ran around their slightly hippy but chic digs. She asked me a few questions. God knows why, she saw a safe bet in me. Maybe it was my naive American enthusiasm. She liked it and hired me as the daytime barmaid.

I would open the pub with Malcolm Addison the bartender at 11:00 a.m. and close at 2:00 p.m.

My first day Malcolm knew he had his work cut out for him: I didn't know shit. I had never even ordered my own beer in London, and in California I wouldn't be able to buy beer or step foot in a bar for another three years. Showing me where everything was, he thought was all that was needed. Bottled beer is here. Baby Cham is here. Crisps are there, three flavors. We get sandwiches delivered every morning, up to you and me to put them out: cheese, cucumber, roast beef, cheese, and tomato.

But then he saw my worried eye drift to the beer taps. Yes, so there, he said, are the beer taps, your Guinness and your lagers. How do I do it? How do you...oh dear...I see. "No time for a lesson now, love, we have to open the doors to business."

Malcolm was as you might've guessed Scottish. Looking back now, he was maybe thirty at the time, but seemed ages older than me. Handsome: dark brown longish hair, mustache, and a twinkle in his eye. And oh the patience of a saint. As he watched me attempt pulling my first pint, I worked that tap like a joystick and beer spilled all over the place. As the construction workers leaned in to watch it soak my shoes. And as I panicked and they laughed, Malcolm calmly came to bring the tap to stillness and showed me how to pull. It would take me at least a week to learn to pour a glass acceptably and the rest of my time there to even come close to mastering it.

It wasn't long before I learned how Malcolm acquired this reserve of patience; he'd been many things in his life, including a brief stint as hash smuggler years before. He had learned to skillfully keep his nerves in check. After that part of his life, he was, "The road manager for Brinsley Schwarz," he said proudly. He could see this meant nothing to me. And I said, finally, "Who's that?"

"What? Brinsley Schwarz, his band!" Nada. He rattled off names of their records. Meanwhile we are pulling pints together for construction workers coming up from the basement covered in dust. "Brinsley Schwarz is why Fred is going to all the trouble of getting the basement up to code. They're the draw. They're the house band. Fresh off a tour with Wings they are."

Pub rock. Now I'm not sure if the term was used widely yet, but the movement was in full swing. In the United States we had no idea it was even happening. By November of 1973, the term was used on air for a Brinsley Schwarz TV performance of "Surrender to the Rhythm on the Old Grey Whistle Test."

The drive of pub rock was simple: let's get back to where we once belonged. In a world of towering amps and gobsmacking stacks of keyboards and overwrought themes and post-psychedelic Floyd and yes even the theatrical costuming of Bowie and Elton—can we just play basic enjoyable rock and do it well and with joy?

In London the summer of 1973, we find ourselves fully committed to a small dedicated little movement in addition to Brinsley Schwarz of a handful of bands; Bees Make Honey, Ducks Deluxe, the Kursaal Flyers, and Dr. Feelgood and a smattering of pubs besides the Hope and Anchor, which you hear about now but the only one I really remember is the Lord Nelson down Holloway Road in Islington.

But no place was more well-appointed to spearhead the pub rock scene than right where I was: getting better at pulling pints, creating Lime and Lagers, and spotting in advance the type of girl who would ask her beau to get her a Babycham. We had Brinsley Schwarz, we had Malcolm, Fred, and Sue, and we had Dave.

Oh…I haven't mentioned Dave yet? Dave lived on the floor directly above the pub. (Fred and Sue lived on the top floor above Dave). Every day just before closing at 2:00 p.m. Dave came down the stairs, wearing a bathrobe, wild brown white-boy afro, and his eyes barely open. He'd stand at the end of the bar and order his wake-up pint. Fred and Malcolm clued me in, "Dave has a recording studio on the second floor. He's going to make records up there." I said, "Dave? Dave who doesn't get out of bed till two p.m.?"

Cheeky little American brat I was. How was I to know that Dave Robinson had been deeply entrenched in the London music scene since Beatlemania. He had tour-managed Van Morrison, Jimi Hendrix, lived with Jimi and Noel Redding, had partied with Jim Morrison, and likely slept with Janis. He was also Brinsley Schwarz's manager.

Maybe it was because I worked during the day, but I never saw any musicians wander into the pub, so for all the talk about

Brinsley Schwarz, I had never laid eyes on any of them. The only musician who ever came in during the day when I was working was Mungo Jerry and oh did he ever make an impression. Elegant, total fox rock star. But I wouldn't know a member of our house band if I served them till closing.

Summer was done and finally so was the construction of the basement. We were all very excited and at the last moment before opening up the live venue again Sue asked if I'd like an extra gig manning the door? I wanted the job sure, but it meant I'd miss the show, 'cause I would have to sit at the bottom of the stairs in the basement and take money and keep the guest list outside the door to the venue. I needed the scratch.

It was cold AF down there in my little hovel. I had to wear layers; my rabbit fur coat, wool stockings, and the tie-dyed scarf Phil bought me for my birthday. Sue brought me drinks and allowed me to get Phil and Tim in free. Fred told me under no circumstances could I let anyone in without paying the five quid cover unless they were on the guest list.

Opening night was insanely packed, we were nearly in danger of another shutdown if I let anyone else in and Fred wasn't about to see that happen. So now my job was more like bouncer than ticket girl: don't let another fucking soul in there. The band was about to go on soon, I gathered from the restlessness of the crowd who sounded well-sauced.

A very tall, thin man with shortish/longish hair (not hippy long, not Bowie short) headed with complete authority into the venue. I was, "AY! You can't go in there. We're at capacity!" He stopped dead in his tracks. And made a slow turn of his entire body and looked at me.

"Unless you're on the list, " I said undaunted.

"I might be." He moved over toward me to check.

"What's your name?" I asked.

"Well now they often call me Speedoo..." When I didn't react, he mumbled, "But ummm my real name is Mr. Earl."

The reference to the Cadillacs classic was completely lost on me, hey man that record was out when I was one year old. So, I took him at his word. Yes, I searched the guest list for Speedoo, and then for Mr. Earl. He waited patiently, "Love, I'm Nick. Lowe. I'm in the band." I looked up to his smiling face and his thumb pointed at the door. My face dropped, "I'm such a dumbass..." He laughed, "Just thorough." Fred was coming down the stairs now, "Nick!"

Nick recounted, "She's good, she wasn't going to let me in." They had a good laugh, and Nick smiled at me, "But I quite like that you thought my name was Speedoo." I laughed and surely blushed. No, sir, to me you will always be Mr. Earl.

Nick persuaded Fred to close up so I could watch the show. My first ever pub rock back-to-basics set in that small crammed room on that little stage. I don't remember what they played, I feel like I heard their cover of "Please Don't Ever Change" 'cause I remember feeling swoony and nostalgic and that song always makes me feel that way.

And I swear they closed the night with "Speedoo." Just for me.

Oh, and that recording studio Dave was building? It became Stiff Records, and Nick Lowe would breakthrough to the mainstream with his seminal albums like *Jesus of Cool*, (initially released in the USA as *Pure Pop For New People*), and *Labor of Lust*, and such genre-defying singles as "So It Goes," "Cruel To Be Kind," "Heart of The City," and "Roller Show," all of which helped to usher in a new wave of power pop that was (hope and) anchored in my little pub rock scene.

Don't ever change, Mr. Earl.

Allison Anders *is an award-winning film and TV director and writer, whose works include* Gas Food Lodging, Mi Vida Loca, *and* Grace Of My Heart. *She's also a former barmaid at The Hope and Anchor and can pull a mean pint of Guinness.*

September Gurls Had It Good

By Rex Weiner

S HE WAS A WELL-KNOWN and highly respected A&R person
at a big record label, and she was hunting for Alex Chilton,
former front man for the Box Tops, who'd topped the charts with
"The Letter" and "Neon Rainbow." The still yet-to-be Big Star was
my friend, neighbor, and one of a group of musicians, poets, and
writers dwelling semi-communally in the five-story Greenwich
Village tenement where the A&R person was standing at the street-
level doorway, pressing first Alex's apartment buzzer, to no avail,
and then mine.

"No," said I, over the intercom—I hadn't seen Alex all day. I'd
just popped some Orange Sunshine, courtesy of an emissary from
the Brotherhood of Eternal Love visiting the East Coast with a
fresh supply. In my youthful quest for Higher Consciousness, or
whatever, I'd decided to indulge that afternoon in a little psychedelic
introspection. Nonetheless, when she asked if she could wait for
Alex in my pad, I buzzed her up, and in the eternity it took for her
to ascend all five flights to my door, the acid began to take hold.
Next thing I knew, she and I were both naked, questing together for
that Higher Consciousness, somewhere over the Neon Rainbow.

Looking back, I thank Alex Chilton for being such a good
neighbor. I can still picture him long-haired on the edge of an

unkempt mattress in his borrowed apartment just below mine, strumming jangly chords on a guitar sometime between 1971 and '73 while Vietnam raged on, Nixon in the White House, Watergate still a third-rate burglary, the world collapsing around us, and nothing seemed to matter anymore except getting high, getting laid—and, hopefully, the music.

December boys got it bad
December boys got it bad

That's how it was, the first time I heard "September Gurls," which novelist Michael Chabon calls "the greatest number-one song that never charted." With shimmering Fender rhythms, Byrds-like harmonies, Keith Moon-ish drums, and a Beatlesque earnestness underlying baffling lyrics, the song's retrospective alchemy creates, for power pop aficionados, the genre's Ur-classic track. For me, it's a subway grating updraft on a warm summer's day, sweet and melancholy whiffs of 1970s New York City, the downtown bar crawls, crosstown tripping, uptown girlfriends, all-around hanging out, young and chasing our crazy muses in directions none of us could have predicted.

But I may be wrong. Maybe his hair was short (mine was definitely long). Maybe it's simply the sound of Chilton's reedy voice I'm recalling, as "September Gurls" wasn't recorded until 1974 on Big Star's second album, *Radio City*, and perhaps it was "Thirteen" he played for me, or some other song; he was always working on something. I liked that about Alex, a midcentury man like me, born in 1950, both of us busy with the future; Alex escaping Memphis and his Box Tops past, just as I was shedding junkie years and the body count of friends lost to drugs and war. Often cited as one of modern music's more contradictory figures—a teenaged two-hit-wonder failing ever after to find commercial success, yet leaving behind a tremendously influential legacy—Alex Chilton sings out from the soundtrack of my own complicated story.

With so much happening then, and so much since, exact details of those days blur. To refresh my memory and piece together the "September Gurls" puzzle, I put in a call to another former neighbor, legendary singer/songwriter Keith Sykes.

"You had the apartment upstairs on the fifth floor directly above mine," Sykes recalls, fixing the location at 231 Thompson Street, a couple of blocks south of Washington Square Park.

His recollection is corroborated by files I've since acquired from the FBI, which was surveilling me at the time because of my publishing an underground newspaper partly financed by John Lennon, engaging in antiwar activities, and palling around with known subversives like Abbie Hoffman and Jerry Rubin. When not overthrowing the government, I was strumming my guitar in Village "basket houses," writing bad songs and trading cool licks with musicians like Sykes and Chilton, who stayed for a while at Sykes' pad downstairs from mine.

I'd reached Keith at Ardent Studios in Memphis, appropriately enough; it's where Chilton and Big Star recorded. Sykes' own song "Coast of Marseilles" is a melancholic masterpiece recorded by Jimmy Buffet on his first album, which paradoxically earned Sykes a spot touring with Buffet's eternally partying Coral Reefer Band. Sykes today is chief manager of Ardent, following the death of studio founder John Fry, and leading a resurgence of the landmark recording facility where John Prine, the Posies, White Stripes, Isaac Hayes, Bob Dylan, ZZ Top, and the Cramps, among so many others, laid down classic tracks. Big Star devotees still show up at the door on Madison Avenue as if on pilgrimage to a sacred spot.

Sykes was among the first southern expatriates to colonize the five-floor walk-up at 231 Thompson. We hadn't spoken in nearly fifty years, but his soft drawl is instantly familiar, his memory of hanging out with Alex a bit wistful.

"We were just exploring life then. We were so young…"

In those days Sykes was just another guitar picker who'd come to New York in the summer of 1968, a Kentucky boy eager to join the folk music scene. Catching the tail end of an era that had spawned Dylan and so many others, he met Jerry Jeff Walker ("Mr. Bojangles"), who lived at 231 Thompson where songwriter Gary White ("Long, Long Time") was also an inhabitant. With a first album in 1969 for Vanguard, Sykes was playing Village venues like the Gaslight and the Bitter End by the time I moved into the building. He had a song I liked about the "Shakespeare of hitchhiking"—I'd done my fair share, thumbing across the country Kerouac-style—with a chorus that went:

> *In the mirror of the sky*
> *Reflects a vagabond*
> *Who's not look'n for*
> *A password to tomorrow*

He sang it "vag-o-bond," not unlike the way Chilton sang "Gimme a ticket for an air-o-plane" on "The Letter," a bluesy twist for a couple of Southern white boys; they had that in common, but were unacquainted until Alex moved into 231 Thompson, subletting from Memphis ex-pat Gordon Alexander.

"Gordon was downstairs below me on three," Sykes says, "which is where Alex was staying while Gordon was away in San Francisco." Sykes reminds me that Norman, the building super, was dealing pot and coke, and rent was seventy-five dollars a month. We speculate that it's probably a lot more than that now.

To fill in more of the details, Sykes surprises me by handing the phone over to Alexander, a Memphis poet and short story writer who, when I knew him, was stenciling his poems all over New

York City subway walls and pillars. He later went on to publish *The Buffoon*, a humor magazine, and wrote about music for *The Dixie Flyer*. Today, Alexander also works at Ardent Studios.

"Yeah, you lived upstairs," says Gordon, "and once when we were carrying on you dropped down a mirror hanging on a string with a note saying *What's going on down there?* We tied a hash pipe to the string and you reeled it back up."

It was the summer of 1971, according to Michael O'Brien, a Memphis-born photographer whose award-winning portraits of people like Willie Nelson and Tom Waits reside in the permanent collection of the Smithsonian's National Portrait Gallery, and other places. His early photography captured Big Star in the band's formational days in Memphis.

"I was working at NYU and lived in the Weinstein dormitory," O'Brien emails me from his home in Austin, Texas. "After I got settled, Alex came up from Memphis and moved in. Vera Ellis, Alex's girlfriend, soon followed. The dormitory was no more than a couple of hundred square feet. Pretty cramped. After the lease expired, the three of us moved over to Keith's apartment on the fourth floor. I guess Keith was on tour. I definitely have memories of 231 Thompson Street! Yes, I remember you living there on the fifth floor. We stayed in Keith's apartment a week or so, when I think an apartment on the third floor came available. We transferred. Alex and Vera had a bed, and I slept on a mattress on the floor, usually under the kitchen table. My most vivid memory is of a huge section of sheet rock falling from the ceiling in the middle of the night. It came right down on top of the table I was sleeping beneath! Once the summer ended, I went back to college at the University of Tennessee in Knoxville. Alex and Vera stayed on."

Yes, I do remember poking my head in there and seeing the mess of that collapsed ceiling, which, like the rest of New York

City in those dark times of municipal bankruptcy, remained unrepaired for a long time. I also remember Vera as a slim, dark-haired beauty, sticking close to Alex. Evidently in love but a little out of place in the big city, they mostly holed up in that tiny apartment downstairs. There was one interlude when I visited them in the Hotel Earle located on the edge of Washington Square Park, a tattered caravansary where Dylan, the Stones, Bo Diddley, Chuck Berry, and a multitude of dope dealers had passed through. I don't remember what Alex was doing there or why I went to see him. That ceiling disaster on Thompson Street may have had something to do with it.

I've read descriptions of Chilton as "enigmatic," but I always thought he was just shy. Sykes disagrees. "He wasn't shy, just thinking, like a lot of writers," he says. Makes sense. Alex was getting $150 a week to write songs for producer Dan Penn, so the guitar was usually in hand when I'd drop by. Or else he'd be at Keith's where they recorded on a TEAC with a couple of Shure mics, and the sound of all kinds of music on Keith's turntable came drifting up to my window. "We were listening to stuff he turned me onto like Moon Mullican," says Sykes, "and Aaron Copland's *Appalachian Spring*. Alex also turned me on to Eric Clapton."

In turn, Keith infused Alex's pop/rock sensibility with rootsier sounds. He recalls showing Alex a Blind Willie McTell song he'd learned from Village folkie David Bromberg, with a riff later incorporated into Big Star's "In The Street," which became the theme song for *That 70s Show*. That the Delta blues found its way onto prime time television via a Columbia University-educated New York Jewish bluegrass musician transmitting it to a Kentucky troubadour who passed it along to a Memphis-born songwriter who grew up closer to the Beatles than the blues was just the way things happened in that fecund time and place.

Jody Stephens, Big Star's drummer, now also working at Ardent Studios as Production VP, gets on the phone next. Alex's musical tastes were always "much broader," he says, and doesn't recall the term "power pop" being applied at the time to what Big Star was doing. "We were just playing music without any direction."

Memphis in those days, for well-to-do white kids of that generation, was at the crossroads of Stax and Lennon/McCartney, and Stephens epitomized that mix. Before Big Star, Stephens had a soul band with his brother, and then a "British Invasion cover band." After Alex returned to Memphis from New York, he joined with Chris Bell to form Big Star, and Stephens came on board. The band played a series of gigs in New York. Venues included Max's Kansas City and CBGB's where I saw the band play and where many of the leading rock critics of the day like Lester Bangs, Richard Meltzer, and Billy Altman fell in love with them. They were all drinking buddies of mine, but when they began hailing Big Star as the new Saviors of Rock, I felt superior to them because I already knew Alex Chilton, and (in my snooty opinion) they didn't understand him the way I did: a deceptively superficial pop rocker tethered by seriously deep roots (and no shortage of hot women coming to call).

"Somebody even called us a punk band," Stephens laughs.

"September Gurls" is anything but punk. "The cool thing about that song," says Stephens, "is that it was so easy to figure out. The feeling...the opening chords—wow." He remembers recording it in Ardent's Studio A, just a few feet from where he's talking to me now. "It was the feeling you have when you're not playing a drum track in a vacuum. It's a pretty remarkable song."

Stephens also recalls the famous image chosen for the *Radio City* album cover by the late, celebrated photographer William

Eggleston, who was a friend of Chilton's parents. Taken at a TGI Friday's restaurant in Memphis, the shot frames a bare light bulb screwed into a crimson ceiling, pale cords running from the fixture beyond the album's corners. "Definitely an unusual photograph, it grabs your attention. You know this isn't going to be a polite record. Everything we did had an edge to it."

Exactly, and I can still feel the optimism of the opening chords colliding with the song's ambivalent lyrics, making "September Gurls" the perfect expression of its murky era. The song captures its young composer in all of his moody contradictions, playing on with ceilings collapsing all around him, making up for early, ill-advised mistakes, the kind many of us make and try our damnedest to learn from. As the progenitor of power pop, "September Gurls" draws desperately on an imagined innocence of the past, even as it reaches hopefully for the future, whatever that might have promised then—or now.

If I could only get Alex on the phone too, we might nail down the details—"Hey, what about the night the ceiling caved in? Wasn't it on that new twelve-string you played 'September Gurls' for me? And while I'm hip to 'I was your Butch,' the lyrics referring to the comic book character, a bulldog who was Pluto's nemesis, according to Jody's explanation in a YouTube video— what the hell is the song about, anyway?"

Not that I'd have the right number, or that he would even have a number, or that he'd pick up the damn phone in any case. Alex Chilton was always hard to pin down. Because—well, never mind, as Alex would say. He's been gone, sadly, since 2010. But rock and roll is here to stay.

Rex Weiner *is a journalist and author whose stories about a detective working in the music industry, serialized in the* New York Rocker *and* LA Weekly *in 1979–80, became the controversial Andrew Dice Clay movie,* The Adventures of Ford Fairlane, *directed by Renny Harlin for 20th Century Fox, released in 1990. Those original stories have been published by Rare Bird Books.*

Wouldn't You Like To Know Me? Paul Stanley's Secret Power Pop History

By Ken Sharp

THIS MIGHT SOUND CRAZY but I'm gonna let you in on a little secret; KISS's frontman, the starry eyed, black leather and studs, seven-inch high heeled boot wearing, Flying V playin', Paul Stanley, is a huge power pop fan. Not only is the guitar destroyin' "Star Child" an über fan of the genre, he walks the walk, and many of his songs, either written for KISS or as a solo artist—"C'mon and Love Me," "Room Service," "Coming Home," "Let Me Know," "Wouldn't You Like to Know Me," "Goodbye," and "Tomorrow"— resonate with the glorious essence of consummate power pop. If you can listen without prejudice to the mighty foundation of Stanley's musical oeuvre, you'll hear echoes of such sixties power pop progenitors as the Beatles, the Who, Small Faces, the Move, the Nazz, and seventies mainstays, Raspberries, Badfinger, and Slade. He's even cited Big Star as an influence in a recent *Rolling Stone* magazine interview.

Back in '77 when it was "uncool" to venture such a proposition, KISS covered the Dave Clark Five's classic, "Any Way You Want It" on side four of *KISS Alive II*, and Paul Stanley didn't need a goddamn skinny tie and smartly tailored matching suit, he's already got power pop coursing through his veins. The former Stanley Eisen christened himself "Paul" after one of the freakin' key architects of power pop, Paul McCartney. Stanley's death-defying onstage acrobatic leaps, slashing windmills and pop-art guitar destruction were heavily influenced by the man who coined the term "power pop," the Who's Pete Townshend.

In 1970, Stanley teamed up with Gene Simmons—another avowed pop fan who later tried to sign Shoes to his Simmons Records label—in a band called Wicked Lester, and signed to Epic Records. While Stanley has uncharitably described the album as "eclectic crap," Wicked Lester's three-part harmonies, inventive arrangements, and impeccable musicianship were far from a musical joke, showcasing a pure pop sensibility light-years away from the heavy metal thunder of their subsequent musical project. Stanley's jaunty banjo driven pop confection "Molly" wouldn't have sounded out of place on McCartney's *Ram*, and Paul and Gene were capable of immaculate Brill Building pop "Too Many Mondays," a co-write with Barry Mann, no less, and a cover of an obscure Hollies song, "We Wanna Shout," whose refrain of "We wanna shout it out loud" would come to be borrowed in 1976 for KISS's power pop anthem, "Shout It Out Loud" featured on *Destroyer*. Of course, fate did not smile on Wicked Lester, but as Paul and Gene reorganized as KISS, Stanley was one of the many fans packing Carnegie Hall for Raspberries' sold out show there in September of 1973. "The Raspberries were absolutely awesome," Stanley told me. "They were so uncool that they were cool. What they did, they did brilliantly."

A year later, KISS's gritty, hard-hitting self-titled debut, nevertheless contained trace elements of power pop, particularly in Stanley's "Let Me Know," "Firehouse" (inspired by the Move's "Fire Brigade"), and the Stanley/Simmons penned "Strutter."

"The beginning of 'Deuce' was me ripping off the Raspberries," Stanley confessed to me. "The thing that starts it off is me bastardizing "'Go All The Way.'"

Subsequently, *Hotter than Hell, Dressed to Kill, Destroyer, Rock and Roll Over,* and *Love Gun,* were all infused with a contagious power pop spirit on tracks such as "Comin' Home," "Room Service," "C'mon and Love Me," "Anything For My Baby," "Tomorrow and Tonight," and "Flaming Youth." Stanley told me that "Love Her All I Can" was "inspired by both the Who and the Nazz, Todd Rundgren's old band. They had a song called 'Open My Eyes' and it's basically the same intro. They copied the Who and we kind of copied them." Even the band's all-time classic anthem "Rock And Roll All Nite," with its explosive guitars, commanding vocals, and criminally infectious chorus, is full on power pop, cut from the same stylistic cloth as hard power poppers, Slade. It was also KISS's first legitimate pop hit and helped rocket them into superstardom.

On December 31, 1974, the Raspberries were invited to open for KISS in Evansville, Illinois.

"Boy, was that a strange bill," Raspberries' Eric Carmen later told me. "It was originally supposed to be KISS headlining with Iggy Pop opening. The tickets had been sold for weeks with that bill. A week before the show, the mayor of Evansville said he didn't want Iggy Pop playing there because he was afraid he'd cut himself with glass and dive off the stage into the crowd and they'd be responsible. Suddenly Iggy was off the bill and somehow we were offered the slot and our management took the gig. The crowd was expecting to see Iggy Pop and we walked out there and they were booing and throwing things at us. Eventually, we got them to calm down and made it through without getting killed (laughs) and maybe even won a few people over. After the show, I remember talking to Gene and Paul in the hallway. They were both very friendly, and Paul said, 'We used to play songs like yours with three-part Beatle harmonies and then this happened.'" (laughs)

Stanley was so impressed with Raspberries records that KISS hired their producer, Jimmy Ienner, to serve as executive producer of their 1978 greatest hits album, *Double Platinum*. Personally, I knew nothing about Raspberries back then, but what I did know was that I gravitated towards Paul's tightly constructed, power charged three-minute songs, so it would appear that my future obsession with Raspberries-like power pop was actually kick-started by the former Stanley Eisen.

In 1978, I was a "KISS freak" at my High School and much to the dismay of many of my classmates, I wore my badge of KISS-mania proudly. Years later, I would go on to pen two official books on the band, *Behind the Mask* and *Nothin' to Lose: The Making of KISS (1972–1975)*.

In an unprecedented marketing move, smacking of equal doses savvy genius and misguided insanity, September of 1978 saw not one, not two, not three, but *four* KISS solo albums. Ace's self-titled release was an unabashed celebration of gonzo Zeppelin/Hendrix gargantuan riffery and generated the only hit single from the four albums, a glam rock fueled cover of the Russ Ballard penned "New York Groove." In direct contrast to his snarling "God of Thunder" persona, Gene Simmons' solo album was a schizophrenic amalgam of Beatlesque pop and groove heavy rock numbers bookended by—I kid you not—a faithful rendition of "When You Wish Upon Star" from Disney's "Pinocchio." Power pop icon, Cheap Trick's Rick Nielsen, guested on a new reworking of "See You In Your Dreams," previously cut for KISS's 1976 LP, *Rock And Roll Over*. Meanwhile, the band's drummer, Peter Criss, alienated many in KISS's fanatic fan base by completely eschewing rock and roll raunch in favor of sparkling blue-eyed soul and Brill Building Pop. But it was Paul Stanley's epic solo album, which lovingly showcased his deep love of Raspberries-inspired power pop. These were anthemic songs bursting with huge melodic guitars, soaring vocals, heavenly hooks, and explosive musicality/commerciality; in essence, with his solo album Paul set aside the muscular machismo hard rock trappings of his band and allowed his true musical self, a passionate and fervent flag-waving worshipper of power pop, to be on display.

Starting with Paul's, I slapped the album on my crappy second-hand Radio Shack turntable and dropped the needle on side one. I loved all four albums: Gene's for its wacky eclecticism with special guests ranging from Lassie to Aerosmith's Joe Perry, Cher to Bob Seger; Ace's epic guitar feast; and Peter's smoldering R&B. But it was Paul's solo album that hit me hardest. Intoxicating hooks, incandescent melodies, and the Who meet Raspberries slashing power chords; more than any KISS album, Paul Stanley's eponymous 1978 solo debut occupied a special emotional place for me. It wasn't until I interviewed Paul years later and delved into the backstory of that album that it would come into focus. "'Wouldn't You Like to Know Me' had some of my little Raspberries licks, my Raspberries steals," Stanley revealed to me, citing Raspberries' "Tonight" and "Ecstasy" as influences. "It's my Raspberries homage."

Now it all made perfect sense. This was Paul's power pop album. Power pop is all about big dumb hooks, irresistible melodies, and loud guitars, and those key elements define the ethos of his solo album and much of his finest work with KISS. Lyrically, Paul's "Tonight You Belong to Me," "Wouldn't You Like to Know Me," and "It's Alright" often straddle the same lyrical territory as such testosterone-fueled Raspberries hits as "Go All the Way," "I Wanna Be with You," "Tonight," and "Ecstasy." They aren't a far cry from the hot-blooded, horn dog lyrical platitudes of songs found on Paul's solo album like sweaty sex is a common thread, conjuring the implicit carnal promise of tonight as an almost mythical romantic rendezvous; *tonight* is the night when it's all gonna go down; that's right, dreams are gonna come true in the backseat of this green Camaro. Groupies also get name checked; Raspberries' "All Through the Night" vows "I'm gonna make you sweat 'til the sheets are wet" while KISS's "Room Service" continues along similar lines with its bad-ass boasts about Stanley's sexual magnetism ("but just when I'm about to shut the light and go to bed, a lady calls and asks if I'm too tired or if I'm just to dead for room service…")

Paul's solo album wasn't his last foray into the jangle crunch kingdom of power pop. By the turn of the eighties, bands like the Knack, 20/20, the Plimsouls, the Dwight Twilley Band, Squeeze, XTC, and the Babys were delivering compact, radio friendly power pop grenades, which reflected the ever-changing musical zeitgeist. Many hardcore KISS fans have written off 1980's *Unmasked* album, accusing the band of selling out their hard rock roots by unashamedly jumping on the power pop bandwagon. But for me, *Unmasked* was KISS's full-fledged power pop album, a terrific record that was simply a natural progression, hot-wired by combustible, melody laced prime tuneage ("Tomorrow," "Shandi," "Is That You?," and "What Makes the World Go Round") with nothing contrived or cynical about it.

The Star Child's one degree of separation frompower pop doesn't end there. Flash forward to November of 2004. After years of persistent demand by their loyal fan base, Raspberries reunited to perform series of well-received shows around the country. The last stop of the tour was at the House of Blues in Los Angeles and not surprisingly, Paul Stanley was in attendance. Before the band came on, a bunch of fans noticed him sitting in the balcony and began loudly chanting his name, "PAUL STANLEY! PAUL STANLEY! PAUL STANLEY!" Don't believe me? On the Raspberries' *Live on Sunset Strip* CD released in 2007, listen closely before the band kick into their first song, "I Wanna Be with You" and you can hear that chant in all its glory. Full circle indeed.

With his work in KISS and as a solo artist, Paul's reverence for power pop music comes across LOUD and CLEAR, whether his fan base were aware of it or not. Turning hundreds of thousands of devoted foot soldiers in the KISS Army on to the wonders of power pop, particularly the Raspberries, might be one of the coolest and most subversive moves of Paul Stanley's over four decades in the music business.

As for me, over the past several decades, my appreciation for power pop has deepened. I've penned/co-penned a number of books on various power pop bands including Raspberries (*Overnight Sensation: The Story of the Raspberries* and *Raspberries: TONIGHT!*), Cheap Trick (*Reputation is a Fragile Thing: The Story of Cheap Trick*), Small Faces (*Quite Naturally: Small Faces*) along with multi-volume celebration of the power pop genre itself (*Play On! Power Pop Heroes*). I've also released five power pop flavored CDs (*1301 Highland Avenue, Happy Accidents, Sonic Crayons, New Mourning,* and *Beauty In The Backseat*).

That said, it's only right that I give mad props to Mr. Stanley for supplying a kick-ass melody-soaked musical road map that helped fire up my interest in the genre both as a songwriter and author. Paul Stanley, massive power pop fan, who'da thunk it?

Musician and *author Ken Sharp has long been a champion of Power Pop, and is the author of many published works on the subject, among them the multi-volume book series,* Play On! Power Pop Heroes, Overnight Sensation: The Story of the Raspberries, Reputation is a Fragile Thing: The Story of Cheap Trick *(with Mike Hayes), plus* Raspberries TONIGHT!, *and* Eric Carmen: Marathon Man *(with Bernie Hogya). As a musician, Sharp has released the original albums* 1301 Highland Avenue, Happy Accidents, Sonic Crayons, New Mourning, *and* Beauty in the Backseat.

Strange Magic: ELO and Power Pop

By Kate Sullivan

I LOVE ELO.

Jeff Lynne's Electric Light Orchestra.

ELO is music that brings an urgent message to the world: *Life is special.*

But ELO gives even more. Their music also says: *Music is special. Music is an event. And isn't it exciting?*

I compare ELO to a passion flower—you know, that crazy flower that looks like a Martian spacecraft crossed with a carnival ride? It's a flower so grandiose and seemingly *designed* that it's more than a flower. It's a flower about flowers. It's a *statement* about flowers that says: *Look at what a flower can be.*

That's why the passion flower is the ELO of flowers. And ELO is the passion flower of bands. Because ELO is *music about music.* Music about the Beatles, and Beethoven, and Roy Orbison, and a thousand other things. (ELO's logo even kind of looks like a passion flower if you squint.) And, of course, ELO is also great music in its own right.

It's music made from pure feeling, and it's music about feelings—massive, intense feelings that require a whole sonic universe to roam about in. In fact, they're so huge, they're actually collective, and ideally involve many people expressing and feeling them together.

What does all this have to do with power pop? It has come to my attention that some people consider ELO to be power pop. ELO is certainly influential on power pop-ish music of the last fifteen years. But ELO isn't power pop per se. ELO is power pop like a narwhal or a platypus is a mammal. ELO has power pop characteristics, but it's so much more than that. Yes, ELO is all about the power. (They're called the Electric Light Orchestra!) Yes, ELO is all about the pop. (They had seven Top 10 hits between 1975 and 1981.) But ELO does not smell or taste like power pop—at least not by traditional definitions. And I think a clear definition is needed. Power pop has enough problems just being recognized as a genre.

My idea of power pop includes the Raspberries, the Knack, Cheap Trick, Dwight Twilley and Phil Seymour, Nick Lowe, Emitt Rhodes, the Beat, Starz, and a thousand other groups. Many are obscure, none are genuine pioneers, and some aren't even that great. It's okay. Power pop is the only rock subgenre whose worst bands are still stylish and entirely listenable. Power pop is also the secret magical ingredient for many platinum acts of the 1980s including the Cars, the Bangles, Rick Springfield, Huey Lewis and the News, and others (all of whom I consider covert power pop bands).

I get the argument that ELO belongs on the power pop spectrum. In the early eighties, they got kinda power poppy— like "Hold On Tight" and "Rock 'n' Roll Is King." Lynne started losing the strings, going more rockabilly, developing the sound that became his signature as a producer for George Harrison, Tom Petty, et al. It's the sound you hear in the Traveling Wilburys. It roams a smaller musical landscape than classic-era ELO, and yeah, okay, you could call it power pop.

But in ELO's rich discography, those records are post-peak highs. ELO's creative heyday is truly the seventies, when they were attempting much bigger things. Just to be fair, though, let's look at some of the shared DNA between ELO and power pop:

1. Heavy Beatles influence
2. Some rockabilly influence
3. Some Byrds influence
4. Music-about-music (see 1–3)
5. Harmonies
6. Pleasing chord changes
7. Hooks aplenty, catchy choruses
8. Fairly simple melodies
9. Romantic themes
10. Guitars, esp. the jangly kind, esp. 12-strings both acoustic and electric (Rickenbackers and such, see 2, 3)

That's some pretty good DNA.

But ELO also has totally divergent influences. They have disco tendencies—they even predicted it in 1973 with "Showdown." Power pop doesn't have a disco bone in its body. ELO has orchestral compulsions; power pop has keyboards, *maybe*. ELO has spiritual vocoders and mystic visions of Shangri-La. Power pop has skinny ties and visions of hot girls chewing bubblegum. ELO has as many mustaches and beards as possible; power pop has none. ELO has lasers, fog, and a spaceship. Power pop has... well, not a spaceship.

Perhaps most importantly, ELO has almost no garage-rock influence. By contrast, the "power" in power pop comes from its band-ness. *It's a band thing.* It's music you can make with three people in a garage (or one, if you're the Toms!). Or else it's a singer-songwriter thing. Either way, it's music that's achievable by young people with low budgets and no violin training. That's part of its charm.

Also part of its charm: power pop doesn't need to travel the cosmos to find existential freedom. Power pop finds thrills aplenty right in its own backyard. I support power pop's affection for the early Beatles. I love that power pop looks so good dressed in black and white. If power pop was a person, and you asked them about their idea of heaven, here's what would happen: They'd think for a moment, and then they'd say, "That scene in *A Hard Day's Night* when the Beatles are playing cards on the train, and they're sitting in that cage, and then suddenly they have their instruments and they're singing 'I Should Have Known Better.' *That's* heaven."

Power pop would be happy to ride that train all night, forever. And why not? That little cage *is* one kind of heaven. It's a portal to the Eternal Pop Now. It's pure joy.

But ELO has a different relationship to the Beatles, and a different karma. ELO was formed as a reaction *against* the "band thing." Lynne says, "That was why we did ELO in the first place—to get away from the three guitars and drums."

As English music maven Alan McGee writes, "When Roy Wood and Jeff Lynne started [ELO]…the manifesto was clear—'Pick up where the Beatles left off'—and for the next eight years, they did exactly that."

Where they left off is key. The idea was never to romp in the early Beatles' creative slipstream. I've read that Lynne didn't even like "Love Me Do" when it came out. His rock and roll epiphany was Roy Orbison's "Only the Lonely," and in its way it provided a foundation for ELO as much as the Beatles did.

In any case, Lynne is much more of a later-Beatles guy, even in his temperament. Like the Beatles, Lynne comes to life inside a recording studio, and ELO is definitely studio music: multitracked and orchestrated as fuck, involving at least three more bodies (and one more spaceship) than could comfortably fit in a touring van.

So for ELO, *Rubber Soul* and *Revolver* are square one, with their demand that rock and roll should be allowed to use any instrumentation or arrangement, and address grown-up themes. And, again, that's just ground rules. The Beatles' concept-album era is where ELO digs in: the full-blown psychedelia of *Magical Mystery Tour* and sprawling everything-ness of *Sgt. Pepper's*. These are ELO's creative stem cells. And it's not just that "Mr. Blue Sky" sounds like "A Day in the Life," or "10538 Overture" sounds like "I Am the Walrus" (though it really, really does). And it's not just the innumerable nods to the Beatles buried everywhere.

There's something deeper—a structural, spiritual kinship. It's the ethos that an album should feel like an event suspended outside of time and normal life, much like a symphony, opera, or film. It's also the ethos that music should borrow/steal from the past (and present) to make something honest-to-God new. That's what the Beatles did with their heroes, and it's what Jeff Lynne did in turn with the Beatles, the Bee Gees (both early and late), Orbison, and his other influences. ELO sought to carry the Beatles' values far into the future—and (yes) into outer space if necessary. John Lennon was a fan, recognizing exactly what ELO was going for. "I call them Son of Beatles, although they're doing things we never did, obviously," he said in 1974. "A statement they made when they first formed was to carry on from where the Beatles left off with 'Walrus,' and they certainly did."

Absurdly ambitious? Absolutely! This is Jeff Lynne. If you don't like crazy-ambitious music, please go back to bed! ELO is rocket-fueled by a kind of creative ambition so aching, exuberant, and brave, ambition isn't even the word for it. It's a thing of beauty,

I tell you! But it's a testament to Lynne's talent that his reach doesn't exceed his grasp by much, if at all. McGee even boldly contends, "It took Jeff Lynne and [ELO] to reach and meet the ambitions of the Beatles template—making their seventies back catalog good enough to match the Fabs."

That's a big, fat polemical argument, but I can't find any holes in it. I shudder just contemplating the fact that *A New World Record* and *Out of the Blue* came out back-to-back in 1976 and 1977. What kind of creative tidal surge could have produced that miracle? It unnerves me even more to consider that Lynne was writing and producing the stuff himself. Of course, we mustn't ignore the contributions of Roy Wood, drummer Bev Bevan, keyboardist Richard Tandy, and bassist Kelly Groucutt—and many others. What they created under Lynne's creative leadership was epic.

That epic-ness is partly why I don't put ELO in the same category with great power pop like the Raspberries or Cheap Trick. Instead I place them in a tent (and what a tent!) with visionary juggernauts such as Queen, Elton John, Wings, the Bee Gees: romantic, expansive artists who were certainly of their time—and knew their way around a string section—but wrote their own rules. Like those artists, ELO created its own species of pop. (And maybe it is or isn't significant that the artists I mentioned are British, and the power pop groups I admire are mostly American. Maybe it has something to do with Ed Sullivan, and the impact the Beatles' TV appearances had on American kids. Maybe Brits had a different experience of the Beatles—a deeper kinship, but less reverent? Seriously, early ELO is like one comedy-degree away from the Rutles.)

Whatever. Over time, Lynne has proven that his relationship to the Beatles goes far beyond being *influenced by them*. And it's more than one-way devotion: It's a back-and-forth where both sides get something from the exchange. Fun fact: In 2019, George Harrison's son, Dhani, guest DJ'd on satellite radio, playing some of his father's favorite records. Along with Howlin' Wolf, Bob Dylan, and the Bulgarian Women's Choir, he played ELO. As Dhani explained, he grew up listening to them, and still remembers that "Telephone Line" was number A-20 in the family jukebox.

George chose Lynne to coproduce his 1987 comeback, *Cloud Nine*, which led to the Traveling Wilburys. Lynne's Beatle-fluency and passion for slide guitar were perfect for Harrison, and their partnership lasted until Harrison's death. As a producer, Lynne even helped the Beatles process their own complex feelings about the Beatles, notably Harrison's "When We Was Fab" and Paul McCartney's "The Song We Were Singing."

And then there's Lynne's work on actual Beatles music. My favorite is the Lennon composition "Real Love," salvaged from a demo (along with "Free as a Bird" and two other songs). When Paul, George, and Ringo needed someone to take a cruddy cassette of John singing at the piano and turn it into a Beatles hit in the mid-nineties, they hired Lynne. They did that for a reason: He's a fucking genius. He's a pro. He's arguably the world's most talented Beatle-obsessive. And, as mentioned, they were ELO fans. (I've also heard that George basically said he wouldn't do the songs without Lynne.)

Knowing how John felt about ELO makes it all the more moving. Fun fact: Lennon also played ELO while guest-DJ'ing (on WNEW in 1974). He praised "Showdown" for its deft hook-thievery: "I'm always nicking little things myself," he admitted, adding, "This is a beautiful combination of 'I Heard It Through the Grapevine' by Marvin Gaye and 'Lighting Strikes Again' by Lou Christie. And it's a beautiful job. With a little 'Walrus' underneath."

That's another reason I don't define ELO as power pop: Lynne's influences range way beyond the Beatles and Roy Orbison, encompassing classical music (obvi), doo-wop, Brill Building/Phil Spector, R&B, soundtracks, myths and legends, science fiction, Disney. ELO never pretended to be music that any kid with a guitar could play. (Did I mention the spaceship?) It's expansive by nature, expensive to record, nearly impossible to reproduce live. That may be partly why more bands didn't copy them until the digital era (although a few did). Digital recording made ELO-ish music more attainable. And guess what? ELO *is* influential on latter-day indie and power pop, as well as some electronic music and arena rock. A few of these artists include: Jellyfish, Puffy AmiYumi, Of Montreal, Air, Daft Punk, Fountains of Wayne, the Flaming Lips, OK Go, MGMT, Fun, Muse, and Weezer. There was even a power pop super group ("LEO") that paid tribute to ELO.

So it's easier to mimic ELO's sonic signatures now. But let's not kid ourselves. There's more to ELO than swooning strings and multitracked vocals. Lynne is a masterful singer-songwriter, and a certain secret sauce goes into his best stuff. It has to do with his very soul—disarmingly relatable, colossally romantic—and his ability to evoke emotion through texture. There's a constant tension between simplicity and complexity: simple lyrical phrases; multi-part choruses that swell and crest on evocative, delicious chord changes. There's tingle-making shifts between minor and major—"Livin' Thing" may be the best example.

These pleasures give a sense of triumph to his lyrics, which are often tragic. *Tragic!* And despite the flawless workmanship, the emotions beneath it are real and magnificently unresolved. Such aching, regret, and loneliness in there. But it's not mopey or boring—this is heroic sadness. (Another contrast!) I call it the Jeff

Lynne Exquisite Longing. It's one of his greatest gifts to me: the infinite beauty of fully realized unfulfillment.

It's in the lyrics, of course. So many upbeat songs about total devastation. And it's in Lynne's voice, which is capable of profound emotional impact. I love the friction of his earthy lead vocals against the precise strings—again, it's a contrast thing. And I know Orbison set the template on "Running Scared," "Only the Lonely," etc., with celestial strings reverb'd to heaven. And T. Rex kinda wrote the book on strings and rock guitars with *Electric Warrior*. But then Jeff Lynne comes along. What's that phrase— genius steals? He took it so far, people think he invented it!

The crescendoing heroic strings of "Big Wheels," reaching up, up, up even as they fall down, down, down. (Are they turning round?) The *Ah-Ah*s on "Telephone Line," bereft and ecstatic, rising and falling like flares in the dark. The plaintive *I'm living in twilight!* Or Lynne's voice on the last verse of "Strange Magic": He moves in and out of falsetto in this way that's heart-wrenching, and also just plain interesting because— again—it's textured. And I could write forever about ELO's guitars, but (again) it's the contrast that gets me, the marriage of sparkling twelve-string acoustics with dark, sinuous, sort of T. Rex-y electric guitars—they're both feeding different and essential parts of my rock and roll soul. Fun fact: Marc Bolan plays twin lead guitar with Lynne on "Ma Ma Ma Belle," which is *so bloody obvious* once you know.

A twelve-string guitar can break my heart. And the gravitational pull of those songs, the weight of the ineffable emotion they contain, is almost planetary. I've gone through long phases where I couldn't even listen to ELO because it just made me feel too much. "Everybody everywhere is gonna feel tonight!" Lynne shouts on "All Over the World," and it's fucking majestic, and absurd, and he means it. ELO can pull me down or lift me up. It's like borderline bipolar.

I should note, in my own personal love story, and mind-heart circuitry, ELO is deeply intertwined with my experience of romantic loss—and rapture! When I've been sad and all alone, depressed and injured, ELO has sung to me in the language of my own heart. Lynne's vision has helped me make sense of overwhelming emotion, or at least given it a poetic structure. It's helped me respect the dignity of heartbreak, and myself as a romantic.

Hey, how you feeling? Are you still the same? Don't you realize the things we did, we did, were all for real—not a dream.

He took the words from my mouth and uttered them into a cosmic megaphone. And with that, I experienced an internal shift. I felt like a little bit less of a loser and a little more of a romantic hero.

So, ELO is sacred to me.

And all that pain gives a keenness to Lynne's upbeat stuff. There's a galvanizing momentum that is so poignant it can make me cry tears of joy—"I'm Alive" (from *Xanadu*), "Hold On Tight," or the George/Traveling Wilburys gem "Heading for the Light." It makes me feel like maybe it's possible to get through this world while actually feeling everything. And not just get through, but even flourish.

I don't give a shit that some people think ELO is cheesy. ELO *is* kind of cheesy—and melodramatic and funny. Woman, he's *seen babies dancin' in the midnight sun!* ELO is attuned to something divine in me and all lovers of love. Humor, absurdity, grandiosity, and real beauty can exist together. They're actually better together.

Passion flower, the flower about flowers, proves this to be true.

And ELO is the passion flower of bands.

Kate Sullivan *is an award-winning journalist and author, and served as the first (and only) female music editor and columnist at* LA Weekly. *Her writing has appeared in* Spin, Rolling Stone, Los Angeles Magazine, Teen People, Seventeen, City Pages, the Da Capo Best Music Writing series, *and* The New York Times Magazine. *She coauthored 2018's* This Is (Not) L.A.: An Insider's Take on the Real Los Angeles, *with a foreword by Jonathan Gold, and she is also an independent radio and podcast producer. Kate has been a fan of the* Xanadu *soundtrack since childhood.*

The Strange Magic of Jeff Lynne

By Tom Petty (as told to Ken Sharp)

JEFF LYNNE CAN PRETTY much do it all. As far as being a consummate artist, he's probably the best all-around musician and singer that I've ever come in contact with, and I've met a few. But he's probably the best at fulfilling those roles. There's not much he can't do musically. I mean I just haven't come across it.

I had been a fan of Jeff's since he was in the Move. Benmont (Tench) turned me onto their album *Message from the Country* when it came out. We would listen to it a lot and go, "Who's this guy Jeff Lynne?" We were really impressed. And then right after that he and Roy Wood moved into the ELO thing. But I was always aware of what he was doing, at least from that point. From the Move, the one that hit me right away was "Do Ya." They did a great version of that track. Why it wasn't a hit by the Move I don't know, but I guess it became one later when he did it with ELO. As for ELO, I like so many ELO tracks. Those songs are so solid. "Can't Get It Out of My Head" is incredible. Just the chords alone to that song are incredible. There's so many. Just as a record *Mr. Blue Sky* is a serious piece of work. I mean, it kind of takes that "I Am the Walrus" thing to another level. It's probably jumping off from that there, but I think ELO kind of jumps off from there. But it definitely became something particular to him and that was a real high point. There's so many great ELO songs; I really like all of them. This guy put out so many hit songs in a row. He's like the one man Beach Boys or something.

Working with Jeff on my first solo album, *Full Moon Fever*, and later with the Traveling Wilburys was kind of mystical. It really began in London when the Heartbreakers were over there playing with Bob Dylan on that European tour. First, when we played in Birmingham, Jeff (Lynne) and George (Harrison) showed up, and we had a little bit of a hang there. Then we went into London and wound up playing for several nights there and George and Jeff came down several times as I remember it. We got to hang out quite a bit in the afternoon, and we all liked each other. We had this kind of instant connection. So it was really strange when I ran into Jeff that day on the road in Beverly Hills on Thanksgiving Day. It turned out that he lived pretty close to where I was living at the time. Then strangely enough, it was either the next day or maybe two days later, I took my daughter out in the car. She wanted to get some Christmas gifts. We were passing this restaurant in the Valley that was kind of a high-end place that we used to go every now and then on special occasions. She said, "Wouldn't it be great to just eat lunch in a place like that?" And I was like, "Sure, c'mon, let's go eat lunch there." So we came in, sat down, and the waiter came over and said, "Your friend is asking for you in the other room." I walked into the other room and it was George and Jeff. George showed me this piece of paper and said, "I just wrote your number down, I just got it from Jeff. Then they told me you were in the next room." So George came home with me, and I don't know where Jeff went. We kind of just spent the rest of the holidays, the three of us hanging out. We played a lot of guitars and sang. The idea of working together just all started evolving from that point with a lot of different things and a lot of different music.

On "Yer So Bad," he helped me with the B-section of the verses, and he came up with a chord or two that really opened it up for me because I didn't really know where to go with it. And I thought, that's great. Then I can't remember how we decided to write some more. But the next one we wrote was "Free Fallin." I sat down at a little keyboard, and I had kind of the main lick, and I think even with that Jeff said, "If you trim a bar off of that, it'll be better," and so I did and he was right. Then I just sang most of the song right off the top of my head, the lyrics and the melody. He was very helpful with the chorus. He had that line "free falling," and I couldn't quite see how it could work. I couldn't get it all in one phrase. But thank God he did. So we finished that up and decided to record them. We recorded those two songs very fast; I think we did them in two days. I remember coming home with those two tracks on a cassette and playing them over and over just saying, "Wow, this is really good." I had to talk Jeff into finishing the album with me because he was about to go back to England for some reason. And I said, "No, no, no, no, we gotta do an album!" (laughs) And he was like, "An album?" And I said, "Yeah, c'mon! We can do it." And so that's how it all started. I kept thinking Jeff was gonna leave and go back to England. (laughs) So it would be like, "Let's go write another one and record it really fast." I think when we finished those first two songs we went into a studio to mix them because he likes to mix things right away and since then, I share that same opinion. I like to mix things right after I do them. I don't like to wait until after the album is done and then try to remember what I wanted. So we thought, okay, let's mix these. While they were mixing them, we went into a little soundproof booth at this studio and wrote "I Won't Back Down." By the time those songs were mixed, we were sitting on another song that we went in the next day and recorded.

Jeff and I got along really well. We had a similar sense of humor. Jeff's a very funny guy. And we were just having fun, which was a kind of new experience for me as far as recording. With the Heartbreakers it wasn't always fun. It would come out good, but it was a lot of work sometimes, and it's just that way with a group. It's a different political arena. So this was the first time I'd ever done anything on my own. Mike Campbell was engineering it, and we were working at his house. It was very informal, and we were just doing it for the fun of it. So I just kept riding it to see how far it would go, and it just kept happening. It worked out really well. We liked a lot of the same music and had a lot of the same influences and come to think of it, really all of the Wilburys did in a way. So that was kind of the common ground between all of us I think. It was surprising when we both realized that we both had done Del Shannon records. We saw a fair bit of Del in those days. He was around and in town, and he'd drop in. George was in town quite a bit too. I remember one night Jeff, George, and I going to some really weird studio in the Valley to see Del. We went in and sang on whatever track he was doing; we did backgrounds for him. It was like that then. It seemed like we were always doing something in the studio.

Jeff was great at sitting down with you and looking at what you had and helping you edit it down or arrange it into something that made it really sparkle. He's a brilliant record maker. He's one of the only people I know that you can go in the studio, and you're gonna leave that night with a record. He doesn't mess around in the studio. He really knows where to go and how to go through a number of options really quickly and find the right one. He's done so much recording ever since he was a kid, it's unbelievable. He really knows what roads are gonna end in a dead end, and he can show you why. He was just brilliant. We did everything on twenty-four-track tape, and we never used more than twenty-four tracks. He was very good at that, helping us get it all on tape. He's just a master. I remember doing some "oohs" and ahs" where we'd roll past the song on the two-inch tape and we'd overdub our harmonies onto there. Then we'd mix them onto a two-track tape and when we had to mix, Jeff would fly them by hand into a track of the twenty-four-track. (laughs) He'd mark it with a piece of chalk, and it might take him two or three tries, but he'd actually hit the button and fly it into the twenty-four-track. It's really delicate stuff (laughs). I'd never seen anything like that before. But with Jeff, it just became another tool in the chest.

It's very important what you don't play. That's a music theory right there being how much of a hole you're gonna leave and how much you're gonna let a note breathe. He was just a brilliant arranger. With me, I tended to kind of hold him back in a way as far as putting a lot of things on the tape. I wanted to keep it very spare. But he just opened my eyes incredibly, and I'm very grateful to him. I mean, the last record we did together, *Highway Companion*, we had a ball doing that record.

Is there a "Jeff Lynne sound"? Well, we're all familiar with the sound of ELO that you recognize instantly and I think that comes a lot from his harmonies, the way he stacks three-part harmonies. He didn't do that much with me because I didn't want it to sound like ELO and neither did he. You notice that sound, it's very commercial, and it's very pop. But when you really listen to it, it's just downright brilliant. I don't know who could do things like that. It's funny because I had wanted Jeff to produce my second album (*You're Gonna Get It!*). I even put in a call to someone and word came back, "Well, he doesn't do outside projects." So I just went, "Oh, well" and went on about my business. But even back then I thought it would be an interesting thing to have him produce us.

With the Traveling Wilburys, I often wonder if Jeff hadn't been there, I don't think it could have been done. The way we worked was very, very fragmented. It was mostly about getting the song written. By the time we had gotten the song written, I think Jeff could picture a lot of the arrangement and how it should go, though you gotta credit George too. Those two were the designated producers of the record, and we knew that everybody trying to produce the record was gonna be a problem. So we all deferred to them, they were the guys that were running the sessions. Jeff was very good at hearing someone play a fragment of something and go, "Wait, wait, wait, that bit there was really good." He had a lot of great ideas. I just wonder if we hadn't had him at the board to communicate with the engineer whether the record could have been made. George did a lot of driving the sessions and deciding who was gonna sing what—sometimes we would record two or three of us singing lead on a track. George would decide which one he wanted to use. Sometimes he might use the bridge from somebody else. It was a very interesting band. (laughs) But I think Jeff's contribution was huge to those records.

When Jeff produced *Into the Great Wide Open*, it was a bumpier road because I think it was probably the only time he worked with a band, and I don't think he really likes it. (laughs) Dealing with the politics of a band just drives him nuts. It can drive anyone nuts and especially them. I think they were a little indignant I'd done a solo album anyway, but I couldn't help but think, "Well, I wonder what would happen if I brought the band in?" And we did and we pulled it off, but it wasn't as easy as *Full Moon Fever*. It wasn't anywhere as easy as that, it was much more difficult. I think Jeff put a stamp in my brain about how you make records. (laughs) There was a standard of record making that I felt like I had stepped up to while working with Jeff. And when I did *Wildflowers*, I felt like I'd done a lot of records with Jeff and I better try to do something else so I can carry on. (laughs) But I still love working with him. He's really my go-to guy on the solo stuff.

When you see that movie about him (*Mr. Blue Sky: The Story of Jeff Lynne and ELO*), and you see him do those songs with just a guitar and a piano, it's just amazing! I don't know who can do that. It's a beautiful thing to just see him play and sing like that. He's singing that stuff present day (laughs), and he's just killing it. I've never heard Jeff sing out of tune. Out of all the recordings and harmonies that we've done over the years, I never once heard him go off-key. (laughs) He's such a pitch freak that he would drive George and I crazy. We did a lot of singing together, the three of us. With Jeff, we always had to sing perfectly in pitch. If it went a little under he'd go, "No, it sounds like the Who." (laughs) And we'd be like, "Oh, okay," and make sure we got it right.

Musician and author **Ken Sharp** *has long been a champion of Power Pop, and is the author of many published works on the subject, among them the multi-volume book series* Play On! Power Pop Heroes, Overnight Sensation: The Story of the Raspberries, Reputation is a Fragile Thing: The Story of Cheap Trick *(with Mike Hayes), plus* Raspberries TONIGHT!, *and* Eric Carmen: Marathon Man *(with Bernie Hogya). As a musician, Sharp has released the original albums* 1301 Highland Avenue, Happy Accidents, Sonic Crayons, New Mourning, *and* Beauty In The Backseat.

Cheap Trick: Power Pop or Just Plain Weird?

By Jeff Rougvie

CHEAP TRICK IS THE band that brought power pop to the masses.

Yeah, I know about the Beatles and the Who and Pete's quote, but that's the embryonic stuff, the Precambrian organisms sliding up the sand from the water. Most power pop fans have hard and fast rules about the genre, although we rarely agree what they are. I personally look for big crunchy guitars (not twee or jangly guitars), harmonies, and hooks.

Much of the music has elements that fans can agree are important, but the musical side of the songwriting is handcuffed by conventional song structure, to the detriment of anyone making an argument in its favor. Only in the hands of true masters are these elements successfully combined and the work becomes transcendent. In those moments, power pop is truly magnificent.

Cheap Trick is truly magnificent, though they didn't set out to be a power pop band. In reality, they were (and still are) America's Greatest Rock Band. But they are also the original ambassadors of power pop, unwittingly masquerading as a mainstream rock band. These things are not binary.

Technology is key in the story of power pop, kids. Rock in the sixties was thrilling, but weedy. In the seventies, technology developed to the point that the studio truly became an instrument, and record producers learned how to properly record the audio elements that came to define power pop—big crunchy guitars and stacked harmonies. Yeah, I know a couple of people figured that out in the sixties, but they were the minority and definitely weren't giving up those secrets.

Not only did Cheap Trick bang out four undeniable power pop records in about two years—starting with 1977's *Cheap Trick* and *In Color*, and ending with 1978's *Heaven Tonight* and *Cheap Trick at Budokan*—but they brought that shit to the masses in a way no power pop band before them had. And let's not forget that *Dream Police* was finished in early 1979, but temporarily shelved to allow the unexpected success of *Budokan* to play out. That's a pretty classic run of top-shelf work in an extremely compressed period, and this from a band that was simultaneously touring its collective asses off throughout.

There have been lots of power pop bands and songs, many long forgotten except by genre enthusiasts. So why are we still talking about Cheap Trick and arguing about their power pop status? Because not only are they great at what they do, but they're proudly weird while doing it.

No one thinks twice about Cheap Trick's image now, but in the seventies, it was revolutionary. Cheap Trick was the band telling bullied suburban teen nerds, "It's okay, we're *ALL* alright." Can you imagine Styx or Journey or REO Speedwagon or Boston being that relatable or ever writing anything as gonzo nutzoid as "Surrender"? Can you imagine any of those bands, charged as the era was with open-shirted, hairy-chested machismo, having weirdos like guitarist Rick Nielsen or drummer Bun E. Carlos in their band?

Like their name-checked contemporaries in KISS, Cheap Trick arrived with a fully formed, completely unique image, but it took both bands a minute to put it across on their album sleeves. KISS finally figured it out on their fifth release, *Destroyer*. Cheap Trick nailed it on their second, *In Color*.

Robin and Tom were the cool seniors from *Dazed and Confused*, intimidating to talk to because they'd seemingly crossed the puberty finish line and were a hit with the girls. But once you got talking to them, it turned out they were alright. Rick was your weird uncle, and Bun E. was some neighbor dad who chain-smoked but never spoke.

Cheap Trick clearly wasn't trying to fit in, but their masterstroke was exploiting that nonconformity. It sent a message of inclusion that only old folkies and the Ramones were selling back then. The difference was that Cheap Trick had a bigger platform and a more accessible sound. Cheap Trick succeeded *despite* being nerdy and weird because they were also *cool* and weird.

It's worth noting that Cheap Trick is from Rockford, Illinois. I've made the pilgrimage to Rockford just to see where they came from. It's technically a city, and has lots of cool stuff, like the Burpee Museum of Natural History (home to the world's most complete T. Rex skeleton; ironically no Brontosaurus, though), but it feels like the suburbs. And even though it's in eastern Illinois' Winnebago County, I'm going to go ahead and say Rockford qualifies as a suburb of Chicago. Cheap Trick is all about the suburbs. And let's face it, the suburbs are weird.

As soon as most rock stars get a few dollars, the standard move is to flee for the big city. Cheap Trick could've gone to Chicago, New York, or Los Angeles, but Rick and Bun E. still live in Rockford. Rockford is in Cheap Trick. Sure, Robin has moved around the area a bit, and Tom lives in Nashville, but they're still hometown boys. There's a Cheap Trick museum in Rockford High School. That's cool AND weird.

And Cheap Trick was inspired by super cool, but often weird, British bands. And not the ones every band cites, like the Beatles and the Who. What makes Cheap Trick different is that Rick read about weird bands in the NME (he had a subscription when practically no one else in America did). He found records by acts like the Move (and their leader Roy Wood), Terry Reid, and Love Sculpture (with Dave Edmunds), many of which weren't released in the States.

So it's no surprise Cheap Trick caused some confusion when they arrived in the mainstream. After roughing it on the Midwest club circuit for a few years, Cheap Trick's self-titled debut (a goddam masterpiece) hit shelves in 1977, a year after the Ramones and the same year as *Never Mind The Bollocks*. This was kinda before punk became a big deal in the US, but just as a lot of first generation punk bands were putting out their debut albums. Also, punk and new wave were frequently lumped together back then (*there's* an argument that rivals "what defines power pop?"), so if your local record shop had a punk section in 1977, Cheap Trick had a 50/50 chance of being in it. It stayed that way at least until *Cheap Trick at Budokan* proved to the heshers that they were a mainstream pop/rock band. Why were they in the punk section? Because the record store staff looked at the covers of those early records, read the song titles and said, "they're weird."

Remember, Cheap Trick came along at the dawn of corporate rock. Album-Oriented Rock (a.k.a. AOR) was a term invented by sixties freeform radio programmers who decided to sell out so they could afford to eat, and then it became an actual genre (more commonly known as Dad Rock). The biggest rock acts in the US at the time were Aerosmith, KISS, Boston, Styx, and REO Speedwagon.

Somehow, possibly because of their omnipresence and the success of *Budokan,* Cheap Trick got unfairly lumped in with the corporate rockers. Cheap Trick never fought to be perceived as part of any genre. Because they're hardworking, practical Midwestern boys, they realized it's foolish to waste an opportunity, so the band welcomed all potential fans and whatever openings fame afforded them. That's admirable, and inclusion has allowed Cheap Trick to have influenced and be revered by acts from all genres. While their Midwestern work ethic makes them one of the hardest working bands to this day, it has led to some weird and inconsistent results.

The core of power pop, the thing that holds it all together, before you add the icing, is songs with great hooks. And Cheap Trick has written a ton of them. But any forty-year career is bound to have some low points. To the band's credit, most of these were the result of disagreements with their label. Furthermore, history shows Cheap Trick was mostly right and the label was often colossally wrong.

Case in point, *Lap Of Luxury,* an album their label's then-new president squeezed out of them after rehabilitating Heart's career in the mid-80s with a load of schlocky songs and some blurry videos. *Lap Of Luxury* is an artistic low point (but possibly a bank account high point) in an otherwise well-intentioned career. They couldn't sound less into it, yet it criminally features their only #1 hit, the completely banal and least Cheap Trick song in their discography, "The Flame." It's weird their only #1 was written by someone else when they have hundreds of songs of their own that are way better and more deserving.

Lap Of Luxury wasn't the first time label interference messed with their recorded output. After pairing them with power pop producer Todd Rundgren (a bad idea from the start, IMO—fight me!), Epic Records famously forced Cheap Trick to record a cover of the Motors' "Dancing the Night Away" before they'd deign to release *Next Position Please*. Decades later, the band got Epic to release an "Authorized Version" of *Next Position* with a rejiggered track list, which is an obvious improvement.

Even though *The Doctor* is a production clusterfuck, there are some great songs buried in the mess, like "Good Girls Go To Heaven (Bad Girls Go Everywhere)." I'd love to tear that sucker apart and rebuild it without the synths and electronic drum sounds because there's real red meat under the tinsel. Except for "Kiss Me Red," a completely uncharacteristic track that Epic (again) forced them to record because the same writers wrote some mostly regrettable power ballad hits. Folks, let Cheap Trick do what they want to do. It usually works out pretty well, even if by accident.

While we're talking about producers of Cheap Trick records, for my money, Tom Werman is the best. To be fair, I imagine many of you agree, but the subject continues to be debated on Cheap Trick message boards long after it should've been settled. Yeah, Jack Douglas kicked ass on the first album, but Werman was at the helm for the magnificent power pop trilogy of *In Color*, *Heaven Tonight*, and *Dream Police*.

In Color is commonly accepted as one of the greatest power pop Classics, but it's also one of the most controversial Cheap Trick records. Fans argue that the production of *In Color* is a few degrees too wimpy, and the band seemed to agree for a time. So much so that, in the nineties, they attempted a rerecording of the album with producer Steve Albini that would rectify the imagined shortcomings. The project was ultimately abandoned, with Zander going so far as to call the exercise "a waste of time."

Frankly, I think a lot of the second-guessing of the album revolves around the studio take of their best-known, most enduring song "I Want You To Want Me." A bonafide power pop classic, Nielsen reportedly wrote it as the Cheap Trick version of an ABBA song—what could be more power pop than that?

Finally, to drive home my point about Tom Werman, remember that after their relationship ended, Cheap Trick worked with the cream of power pop and rock producers including the aforementioned Rundgren, George F'in Martin, Roy Thomas Baker, Ted Templeton, and more. There are some killer Cheap Trick albums as a result, but none quite as magical as the Werman records. Nothing against any of these gents, but if I'm about to die and the last record I get to hear is *In Color* or *All Shook Up*, sorry, Mr. Beatles, you lose.

As the music industry has tumbled into free fall, Cheap Trick stays relevant by still making deliberately weird records, full of idiosyncratic identifiers like the intro to "This Time You Got It" on the underrated *Rockford*, a late period masterpiece and their penultimate studio album with Bun E.

But those are just the studio albums. They're the band I've seen live more than any other and they never phone it in. Even though their touring opportunities over the decades probably look like the cardiogram of a teenager having a heart attack during his first fuck. I've seen them headlining stadiums, county fairs, festivals, casinos, free outdoor gigs, tiny clubs, suburban theaters, the occasional corporate event, and opening for other bands at stadiums.

In fact, the best shows I've seen them do were at career low points. One of the all-time best was in 1986, a year after the release of *Standing on the Edge*. That record was something of a commercial comeback with a top ten single, yet here they were, in Shakopee, Minnesota, at the Valley Fair amusement park. No doubt they recognized it as straight out of Spinal Tap, but they blasted through two (TWO!!) great, high-energy shows, opening the second with a fantastic, knowing version of "Highway To

Hell," a song that perfectly framed their situation at that moment, but didn't diminish the sheer joy of the performance.

Robin is arguably the greatest rock singer ever. He doesn't have the high-end vocals of Freddie Mercury or the growl of Lemmy, but he can cruise comfortably and credibly between the two, and his phrasing is second to none. Yeah, that voice may have lost a little at the high end in the new millennium, but he still hits notes others can only dream of, never mind singers of his vintage. Rick is a songwriting savant whose subversive, oddball arrangements and thick, chunky guitar sound made them unique.

If they weren't so gifted, so perfectly balanced, so beautifully weird, Cheap Trick could have ended up like so many other power pop bands. They might've been nothing more than a cult act that got dropped because their records never sold, played regionally for a few years until they broke up for good, occasionally reuniting for high school reunions or whatever.

Folks, Cheap Trick has been challenged and possibly even tormented by clueless labels, managers, band members, sleazy promoters, sneaky merch guys, ex-wives, and who knows what else, yet they're still here. As impossible and unlikely as it seems, one day there will no longer be a Cheap Trick playing a ridiculous schedule of dates every year. That's maybe the weirdest, most unimaginable Cheap Trick thing ever, but it's inevitable.

So allow me to gently remind you to pay tribute to the Kings of Power Pop and the Greatest American Rock Band while you can. They've earned it by doing what they do best, making great, hard-rocking power pop, with awesome hooks, fat guitars, weird lyrics, and that great voice. More importantly, they've done it consistently, with quality control and seriously goofy enthusiasm. See a show, buy one of their records, send them a message of appreciation. You'll be glad you did.

Jeff Rougvie *is a lifelong power pop fanatic and the writer of* Gunning For Hits, *a crime thriller comic book set in the music* business. *An award-winning producer, he's worked with Badfinger, Big Star, David Bowie, Elvis Costello, Material Issue, Morphine, Bob Mould and Sugar, Jeff Whalen, and many more. He owns the boutique label Supermegabot Music Concern, does expert witness work for music business legal matters, and is currently writing a history of the ground-breaking indie label Rykodisc.*

Power Pop, Peaches, *and* Parallel Lines

By Heather Havrilesky

IN AUGUST OF 1984, on a long car trip across the country with my dad, I listened to Blondie's *Parallel Lines* approximately fifteen million times. I listened to the cassette tape on my five-pound Walkman with the spongy headphones every waking hour of every day for three weeks straight. I was traveling in a rented Oldsmobile with my dad and his girlfriend (nickname: "Peaches") and my older sister and older brother. The only time I wasn't listening was during the few minutes right after my dad yelled at me to take off my headphones and look at the scenery whizzing by my window.

"Stop being so shallow!" he'd bellow into the rearview mirror at me.

My dad was fixated on my shallowness that summer. It's true that I had brand new contact lenses and a new pair of very cheap imitation Ray-Bans. It's true that I wore a bathing suit with thin bubble-gum-colored stripes on it every day, along with a pair of cut-off jean shorts. I was fourteen years old and the atmosphere around me had shifted. I had gone from being adorable to being something else, something more dangerous and less cute. My dad didn't like it, but I did. I liked it a lot.

I know a girl from a lonely street,
Cold as ice cream but still as sweet,
Dry your eyes, Sunday Girl.

In every song on *Parallel Lines*, Deborah Harry walked a thin line between adorable and dangerous, pretty and dirty, coy and vengeful, sweet and merciless. Her voice went from cheerful and sugary to gravelly and morose and back again every few minutes. The fact that I stumbled on this cassette tape at all was an accident: it was part of my dad's collection, which included Mozart, Tchaikovsky, Billie Holiday, the Rolling Stones, the Pointer Sisters, and Devo. I found it rattling around in the console of the Oldsmobile with his other tapes one morning. I was desperate for something besides my five cassettes: three Led Zeppelin, two Police.

Blondie was a revelation, one that unfolded slowly over my first dozen or so listens. At first, the music and the lyrics seemed too simple and pop-like for my taste. But unlike Robert Plant or Sting, Deborah Harry wasn't self-serious and melodramatic about her place in the world. She wasn't straining to be gritty or filthy ("Squeeze my lemon…") or cloyingly intellectual ("We are spirits in the material world…"). Every word she sang had a sarcastic edge to it: *I love this song, but it's also really fucking stupid*, her voice seemed to say. *I'm shallow, but it's funny. I'm as stupid as you want me to be. Let's pretend I'm an idiot, just for fun. Let's pretend I'm as empty as you assume I am.*

You, you with the comb
You look OK in every way, mmm
I, I should've known
You'd look at me and look away. Oh!

The reigning worldview of *Parallel Lines* was a perfect fit with my state of mind that summer. Suddenly, it seemed possible to swerve off the path prescribed for me by my decidedly unshowy, allergic-to-vanity, shallowness-averse family. I didn't have to take myself seriously and get defensive like my sister or brother did. I could be a flashy dipshit if I felt like it.

Power pop had essentially the same vision quest: to be simple, to flirt with emptiness, to try it on for size. *Let's not overthink things, like fucking Jethro Tull or Yes,* the architects of power pop seemed to say. Let's keep things extra fucking simple, but not like the Monkees, not a confused *imitation* of something adorable. Let's be complicated but pretend that we're not. Let's be dour but pretend we're giddy. Let's take something heavy—strong, powerful—and make it bubbly and upbeat.

So that flimsy white plastic tape with the tiny black song titles on it lived in my Walkman, slowly winding forward as we sailed down the highway *(Like a rocket to the ocean, we can run!* as Blondie put it in "11:59"). My dad and siblings had picked me up at the beach where I'd just fallen for a cute boy I didn't know. It had been raining all week, and my friend Carrie and I had run into this kid and his friend in the hallway of her parents' beach condo, all of us looking around for something to do. All week, we would stand around in the hallway together, cracking jokes and mumbling about nothing for a few hours. Then we'd leave, and Carrie and I would high five over our amazing fortune, that no other girls were around.

I didn't know this guy at all, but I felt certain that we would've fallen in love with a little more time. He liked me, I was sure of that. We didn't speak to each other alone or kiss, and I didn't have his phone number. We said goodbye without fanfare, and then I spent the next two months daydreaming about him around the

clock while listening to Blondie. It was hard to imagine things
he might say to me, because I barely knew him. All I knew was
that he was hot. That was enough. It was empty and stupid and
delicious and hopelessly shallow. *That was the whole point.*

> *All I want is a room with a view*
> *A sight worth seeing, a vision of you*
> *All I want is a room with a view*
> *I will give you my finest hour*
> *The one I spent watching you shower*
> *I will give you my finest hour.*

In "Picture This," Blondie offers casual justification for
emptiness. She made it sound rational, the notion that watching
some hot guy shower could amount to your peak experience in
life. Maybe that was empty, and maybe it wasn't. It didn't matter
either way. Her stance was perfectly aligned with the central
dictate of power pop, which was: *Why overthink this? Let's not
take ourselves too seriously. Only tools do that.*

In some ways, my dad enforced this philosophy in the rolling
microcosm of our rental car. In the early afternoons, he liked to
play a quiz game where he'd fire questions at us and everyone
would get ranked from Smartest to Dumbest based on how well
they did. He'd ask questions like, "Who said, 'Don't fire until you
see the whites of their eyes'?" and then my sister or brother would
answer correctly, and Peaches or I would get it wrong. Then
my dad would summarize the results: "Okay. Laura is still the
smartest, Eric is the second smartest, Heather, you're the second
dumbest, and Peaches, you're still the dumbest."

After a few minutes of this, Peaches would glare out the window
and announce that she didn't want to play anymore. Peaches had
blonde hair and sometimes conjugated verbs incorrectly, but

beyond that, she didn't seem that dumb. The dumbest thing about her, in my view, was that she got defensive when she was being openly mocked. That was weak in my opinion. Deborah Harry was cool enough to know that, for a woman, being mocked was just part of the texture of being alive. But Peaches was nothing like Deborah Harry.

This was also where power pop and punk went hand in hand: Both actively chose to be seen as the dumbest. One was cheerful about it, the other was angry. Or as Harry sings in "I Know but I Don't Know":

I know but I don't care
Then I know but I don't see
Now I see but I don't know
I care but I don't care

That cheerful punk nihilism reminded me of Devo (*We Are Devo* came out the month after *Parallel Lines*). But it extended to the most popular song on the album:

Once had a love, and it was a gas
Soon turned out had a heart of glass
Seemed like the real thing, only to find
Mucho mistrust, love's gone behind

In my imagination, Harry was unflappable. If she was secretly neurotic and second-guessed herself constantly, she had the good taste to do it behind closed doors. "Once had a love, and it was a gas" was such an effortful understatement: *Love is amusing but not much more.* "Mucho mistrust" was such a casual way of waving off betrayal. "Poof! Love's gone before you know it," Harry sang breezily, sounding like she just woke up from a long nap, or just nodded off from a long dance with heroin. Her tone was laconic to the point of contempt. *I woke up just for this?*

Harry might've laughed at being named the dumbest. Or she might've played along. "I'm the dumbest again!" she'd sing in her scratchy voice, but the joke would be on you.

◆◆◆

By the time we got to the Grand Canyon, Peaches' nerves were starting to fray. What could be worse than traveling with three teenagers and their father, everyone disrespecting you at once? She stopped chatting cheerfully quite as often and spent long stretches in the front seat of the car, staring out the window at a blur of dry bushes and red dust and cornflower-blue sky.

Likewise, after about ten million listens, all of the simpleton crush-focused pop of *Parallel Lines* flipped on itself, and its edges started to point outward. Even the album cover reflected this: the men in the group are smiling and look the same in their black suits. Harry alone is frowning, in a white dress, her hands resting defiantly on her hips. "Men are all the same," her stance tells us. "Men are a nice background, a pleasing view, but not much more. Don't overthink it."

The craziest and most unexpected song on *Parallel Lines* had to be "Just Go Away," which sounds like it was pulled straight from the *Hair* soundtrack. The yelling in between lines is lifted straight from "I'm Black / Ain't Got No."

Don't go be bad
'Cause you been had
Don't go be sad
Don't go away mad
Just go away

I mean, wow. "*Don't go be bad*"?! You have to admire the *sheer commitment* to being the dumbest that's baked into that line.

Speaking of dumb, we didn't take a lot of water on our hike into the Grand Canyon. There was supposed to be water at the second oasis, but we couldn't find it, so we headed back up the trail in ninety-degree heat, miserable and very thirsty. Peaches sang "Whistle while you work" as we hiked, and shouted things like, "It's okay, guys, we're doing great! We can do this!"

At first, my dad didn't say anything, but I knew he'd break down eventually. After about ten minutes, he told Peaches to shut the hell up. Peaches snapped back that she was just trying to keep everyone's spirits up. My dad said it was annoying. So Peaches stormed up the trail alone, ahead of us, and my sister laid down in the red dust and cried.

Don't go pre-fab
'Cause you been had
Don't go be sad
Don't go away mad
Just go away

Don't show me your feelings, fool, Harry told us. *That's not how we do it.*

◆◆◆

YEARS LATER, I FINALLY figured out that my parents were just as shallow as I was when they were young. I found some old photos of them together, my dad looking like Elvis on the beach without a shirt; tan and swarthy and flexing his pecs, my mom looking like Ann Margaret, voluptuous in a white bikini with a floppy hat, posing like a pin-up. My dad had been singing "You're so vain" to me as long as I could remember, but there they were, a couple of wannabe movie stars, with matching good looks and swagger. My parents weren't the thoughtful, self-serious types who shunned skin-deep ego rewards after all. They were deeply invested in their images. They cared about getting attention. They wanted to matter, even when they were pretending to be above it all.

I was sort of excited to see what a babe my mom was, in the old days. But my dad made me angry. Here he was giving me shit for being vain and shallow all those years, when he was exactly the same way. That's when I started to notice that boys and men can be shallow and instead of being scorned for it, they're applauded. Somehow, even their shallowness makes them deep. Being a shallow dude armed with some raging hormones and a few alternative guitar tunings meant being seen as some kind of an icon or legend. When men were deathly serious about their emptiness and their cravings, it didn't make them foolish. It made them rock philosophers, rock gods.

But I didn't realize that back in 1983. I was well on my way to seeing myself as silly and execrable, as directed. I would undercut my feelings and opinions with humor. I would avoid taking any strong stands. I would bathe my convictions in cynicism, so as to not appear too earnest or naive. I would roll my eyes like Deborah Harry, but when anyone implied that I didn't know enough, I would agree heartily. Better to play along. Better not to look defensive, or invested, or vulnerable. Better to hedge. Better to bite your tongue. Better to hold back. Better to hide.

Hurry up, hurry up and wait
I stay away all week, and still I wait
I got the blues, please come see
What your loving means to me

A girl can win your attention at first, but then she must wait passively for your love and approval. If she's too assertive, if she does what she likes, she gets called shallow. So she hangs back, waiting. Oops! Waiting is shallow, too.

But it's easier for the world to view us as shallow. No one wants to look at how rich and complicated and conflicted women are, how formidable we become before we even recognize it ourselves. Instead, our feelings and opinions are treated as if they're beside the point. Blondie's simplicity seemed to embrace this reality, but Harry always seemed to hint that the truth was murkier and darker than it appeared.

So how do you go from being sweet and cold, suspended, a question mark, to being hot and sour, an exclamation point? Rage, motherfuckers. Disappointment and longing and pure, raw rage. It only took me three decades to land here, but now I realize that I was never shallow at all. I was an ocean all along, vast and unpredictable and dangerous.

Heather Havrilesky *writes the popular advice column* Ask Polly *for* New York Magazine's The Cut. *She is the author of* Disaster Preparedness *(Riverhead, 2011),* How to Be a Person in the World *(Doubleday, 2016), and* What If This Were Enough? *(Doubleday, 2018). She has written for* The New Yorker, The Atlantic, The New York Times Magazine, *and* NPR's All Things Considered, *among others and was* Salon *TV critic for seven years. She lives in Los Angeles with her husband and a loud assortment of dependents, most of them nondeductible.*

The Agony and the XTC

By David Yaffe

ORIGINAL PUBLISHED IN THE Paris Review, *February 22, 2018*

THERE WAS A TIME when you thought you could bury your secrets in a music collection. You were young, you were sensitive to judgment, and you weren't sure how all of it would stack up in the eyes of a potential romantic partner or the mature, sophisticated self you aspired to become. Were you really that needy? That desperate? And would you be crushed if someone else didn't get it? Music got to places that were so private and strange, it was hard to put them into words, at least until you got older.

Supposedly, you now live in a less lonely world. Now you can find refuge in social media, on a fan site, and discover that your little aural secret belongs to other people too. And if the repressed is returned and you reexamine where those sounds came from, you can find that some of those grown-ups who made the music you hoarded were even less stable and sure of themselves than you were. The band I am speaking of is XTC, who are now, despite their general absence from the conversation, the subject of the recently aired Showtime documentary *XTC: This Is Pop*. They were perhaps best known for their accidental 1986 hit, "Dear God," a manifesto of unbelief initially buried on a B side before disc jockeys at college radio stations flipped the record and discovered something that hit a nerve among the young. And yet what was truly terrifying about the song was its harmonic beauty, the way those descending notes and glorious extended vocal lines followed the chords and made its blasphemy somehow numinous and sublime. By the time the record came out, those of us who were following its singer and author, Andy Partridge, knew that while he sounded invincible on the record, he had in fact stopped performing a few years earlier, in 1982, due to a kind of incurable stage fright. This was long before the Internet, and we had to search hard for the information. That voice, filled with angst or tenderness or both, just couldn't make it to the concert stage anymore. The music that was the most precious to Partridge was also somehow unbearable. A few years ago, he appeared on a BBC documentary singing the praises of another head case, the mighty Judee Sill. But when he began to play her song, "The Kiss," he had to stop. "Those notes climbing under her voice... Sorry; I can't do it... It's just too beautiful."

In the early, rowdy days of XTC, it was not obvious that Partridge was one to weep at records. The group started as an often dissonant punk band who found their path into melody by way of maturity. In 1982, when the band was on the cusp of mainstream success, Partridge, suffering from sudden Valium withdrawal, walked offstage in the middle of a performance of "Respectable Street" and stopped performing forever. For the rest of their career, XTC was a studio-only band. The focus would be on playing, listening, digging deep, and truly becoming themselves—including that space of vulnerability that would go straight to your speakers. They would take over a studio like a trio of Stanley Kubrick and not emerge until they poured everything they had into it. There were no shows to prepare for. The records were the shows.

Partridge could have been broken, but he has miraculously survived—a living figure of cult. He spent his career being, at turns, cheeky, angry, edgy, soft, sacrilegious, a father, a drinker, an ex-husband, a weirdo, a crank, an anachronist, an agoraphobe, and so on; etching out, often with great tumult, something that's just too beautiful. His voice, when edgy, can sound like what he describes as "a seal's bark." When it's sustained, it is a thing of wonder, sometimes taunting, sometimes joking, sometimes a long multitracked journey into desperation, loneliness, or an off-kilter bliss.

In *XTC: This Is Pop*, the members of the band are there, as are Stewart Copeland, drummer for the Police (for whom XTC opened back in the day), and Harry Shearer, who cowrote and starred as the bassist Derek Smalls in *This Is Spinal Tap*. It is astonishing to see Shearer, bassist for the most legendary parody band ever, gushing about XTC's "gorgeous songwriting and gorgeous record making." A running joke through this rock documentary is that Andy Partridge really hates rock documentaries.

XTC is pop that is somehow beyond the limits of pop. There is pop and art, and there is rock and art, and yet the terms *Pop art* or *art-rock* don't quite fit. In the seventies, bands such as Yes; Emerson, Lake & Palmer; Genesis; Jethro Tull; and more were known—with their long solos, long tracks, and grandiose concepts—as art-rock. *Pet Sounds* and *Sgt. Pepper* preceded them, and Radiohead's *A Moon Shaped Pool* followed. In the middle was punk, which ripped apart the pretensions of the art-rockers and put Andy Partridge in an awkward position. He couldn't show his soft side, and he couldn't do anything that stretched the listener's attention span. But from his earliest records, what was unmistakable was the chromatic harmony, a concept that sprang from nineteenth-century Germany, starting with Wagner's

Tristan chord. To put it less technically, Partridge's chords are often weird—stacked, suspended, and eerily cast—and they sound like no one else's.

Andy Patridge works through metaphor and synesthesia. In *XTC: This Is Pop,* he walks us through the composition process in real time. He hasn't set foot on a concert stage since the year *E. T.* was released, yet he can still show us how it's done. He takes us back to when he needed to come up with a verse for "Senses Working Overtime." The chorus is in E. Searching for something more interesting, he tells us, he threw his hands "on kind of an E-flat place," but then, without thinking, he wound up with "an interesting chord-nonchord." The sound has an eerie dissonance with just a trace of euphony. "This sounds medieval. This is like somebody in a field, tilling," he says. The song is about being overwhelmed—too much beauty, too much ugliness, too much everything. This was the year of his breakdown. And it was a hit.

On-screen, he explores the guitar frets. "Let me find a chord I've never played in my life," he announces. He doesn't name it, but it's an augmented C-sharp chord. Then he floats along the frets. "That to me suggests a pool of muddy water," he says. And then he starts plonking some distinctly Andy chords, which come with that voice reaching out to us yet again. "There is the muddiest of water / There is the deepest of pools."

It was those Andy chords that first leapt out to me as a teenager, listening to music in the dark. Joni Mitchell's *Blue,* Van Morrison's *Astral Weeks,* and *Relaxin' with the Miles Davis Quartet* were supplemented by XTC's *English Settlement* and *Skylarking.* Those albums were among the first purchases for my CD player. The new technology promised a bright, sparkling future for music, a place beyond the crackles and skips of vinyl. I could hear those stunning intervals, those droning vocals, the meta-psychedelia, the anger, the tenderness, and the strangeness that made it hard to transcribe the music precisely to the piano keys. I was playing jazz, and this pop with harmonic aspirations expanded my eclectic young palate. I was in my first romantic relationships; where pleasure was mixed with pain, joy was laced with acid, and the chords clashed. Music, of course, was often playing through it all.

Some music stays with you for life. It means different things at different times, but it is always with you, like a limb or one of the five senses working overtime. But sometimes it will be years since you last heard, say, "1000 Umbrellas." You've lived several lifetimes since then, and, oh, isn't it magical that some chords can take you back to who you used to be? Except they can't. Your life is not a straight road. But the veneer of continuity—through other people's music, through their feelings, *their* illusions—keeps the jukeboxes playing. You don't get that experience back, but you get a reminder that it is gone forever. The reconstruction of the past is an addictive drug. We want that feeling again, even if it's mixed with inconsolable misery. Andy Partridge had a breakdown for his own reasons, yet we experience it with him every time we listen to him. He went bonkers just for us, didn't he? XTC have been defunct since the beginning of the new millennium. But for a long time, they existed only on records anyway. Even when they came out with a new album, the music was never live. We are lost to ourselves, lost to our pasts, and yet, when confronted with their archives and our own, there is still something recognizable. That's me you think. Or it was. That whelp comes up, those uncanny chords. The dead have been awakened once more. We are at a loss. The tears well. "It's just too beautiful."

David Yaffe *is a professor of humanities at Syracuse. His latest book,* Reckless Daughter: A Portrait of Joni Mitchell, *was published by FSG last October.*

Thanks for Dancing: Tommy Keene and Other Places that are Gone

By Dave Holmes

Iᴛ ʏᴏᴜ ᴋɴᴇᴡ ᴀʙᴏᴜᴛ Tommy Keene, one of the things you knew was that more people should have known about Tommy Keene. It was part of the story with him, the greatest rock star nobody had heard of. It was crucial to the appeal, too. You got to introduce people to him over and over again throughout your life. You got to repeat the process of meeting a new person and deciding whether they were worthy of being let in on the secret. You shared the joy with those who got it, and silently disapproved of those who didn't. You were like an evangelical Christian, except your savior wore pegged jeans well into his fifties.

Certainly more people should have heard Keene's major-label debut *Songs from the Film*, and its follow-up EP *Run Now*. They were on *Geffen*, for God's sake, and the reviews were uniformly glowing. Tommy performed "Run Now" in the classic Anthony Michael Hall action thriller *Out of Bounds*, which would have been a career boost if even one person had asked for an Anthony Michael Hall action thriller. He got a big feature in the first episode of *120 Minutes* in 1986, before even *120 Minutes* knew what *120 Minutes* was. (I know this because I watched it live, taped it, and reran every one of those minutes over and over: at first, the show was a repository for the videos on MTV's light rotation, regardless of genre. That's why the Tommy Keene feature is nestled between Janet Jackson's "What Have You Done For Me Lately" and Jean Beauvoir's "Feel The Heat." 1986 didn't really know what it was either when you get down to it.)

More people should have heard Tommy Keene, but for a million reasons having everything to do with the capriciousness of the record industry and nothing to do with passion or beauty or heart, they didn't.

I owe everything that's good in my life to the fact that I did.

My relationship with Tommy's music began when I read his name in a 1986 issue of *Rolling Stone*. As I recall, the magazine's positive review of *Songs from the Film* name-checked Marshall Crenshaw, whom I loved, and Big Star, whom all the artists I loved loved. That was enough for me to take a chance and drop my allowance on the cassette, which I would have to replace that same year because I had played it so much the sound had become muffled. And then again a year after that. As I recall, Geffen cassettes were clear and smelled faintly of cherry air freshener when you first opened them, and I'm going to need that flavor of scented candle on my desk *stat*.

I was fourteen when I fell in love with Tommy Keene because for the first time, I heard my feelings coming through a speaker. The exact moment when I began to feel like I may be somehow unlike my peers was scored to "I Don't Feel Right At All" and "They're in Their Own World." The summer I began to connect with other artsy teenagers, the lines I kept coming back to were from "Places That Are Gone": "Back before you knew me well, I was trapped inside a shell." Tommy was writing from a place of solitude and longing, of alienation mixed with hope. Like me, he was on the sidelines, observing, knowing there was something fundamentally different about him. Maybe not even being able to put a name to it.

Among other things, Tommy instilled in me a lifelong hunger for local record stores. Once I'd digested the stuff I could get my hands on at Camelot Music, I needed to dig deeper for those *Places That Are Gone* and *Back Again (Try)* EPs, the ones that had topped the Pazz & Jop critics polls in the New York free weekly I'd never actually seen. When I'd visit my brothers in college and graduate school, I'd beg them to take me to the cool part of town, and like Linus searching for the most sincere pumpkin patch on Halloween night to await the Great Pumpkin, I'd scope out the scruffiest-looking vinyl shop where I was certain I'd cop them (or, because I am nothing if not optimistic, a copy of *Strange Alliance*). From 1986 to the present day, I have been regularly acquainted with that special pain caused by flipping from Keel's *The Right to Rock* to Kick Axe's *Rock The World* with no Keene in between. (Fun fact: Every used record store in the world still has multiple copies of both of these albums, such was the irrational exuberance surrounding heavy metal in the mid-1980s.)

He came to my hometown of St. Louis in 1987, just after *Run Now* was released. My brother drove me and my friend Kim—the only other person in my world back then who got it—down to Mississippi Nights on Laclede's Landing to see him. It was an all-ages show, but everyone besides the two of us was over twenty-one, clinging cautiously to the bar. Kim and I danced ourselves right up to the edge of the stage, swaying ecstatically to what you cannot really call dance music. Tommy wrote "thanks for dancing" on the show flyers we asked him to autograph when he came up to us after the show. The man who made music that made our hearts soar ended up being a really friendly guy.

That we were the only two people up that close ended up being part of the appeal. He should have been huge, but he wasn't, and because of that, if you loved him, you felt necessary to him. He was an underdog, even more so than the other artists the artsy kids liked. The Replacements and REM were starting to get top-40 airplay in the late 1980s, but Tommy stayed underground. His second major-label album, *Based on Happy Times*, didn't change anything, but its first track "Nothing Can Change You" gave the world some frank and solid advice—"Stop falling in love with everything that lets you down"—that would have dramatically altered the course of my twenties if only I'd taken it to heart. The Goo Goo Dolls ended up covering that song at the height of their popularity, which goes to show that Keene could have had mass appeal. If you loved him like we did, you wanted more for him, but honestly, selfishly, the fact that he stayed ours felt pretty nice.

Tommy and Kim and I all ended up being queer, which makes a lot of sense. In his lyrics, there was that sort of vague, dull ache that we share—that sense of never being quite at home. I come back to that line "Back before you knew me well, I was trapped inside a shell," which describes coming out, whether he meant it to or not. A lot of his fans were LGBT too, never quite at home with the music the gay mainstream served us, picking up instinctively on what Keene never explicitly said in his lyrics.

There's a restlessness, a search for home throughout his work. But for those of us who loved him, there was a feeling of home at his shows. In my early adulthood, if he was playing anywhere within a couple hours of New York, I was there. A lot of other guys were too. Most of us came alone. A lot of them had memorabilia for him to sign, which he did. A power pop show can look a lot like a comics convention in this way.

Songs from the Film was released on CD in 1998, by which time I was working at MTV. I managed to sneak a mention of the album onto a live show because this was a time when you might expect to find people talking about music on MTV. He played Brownies in New York shortly thereafter, and after the show his tour manager waved me over. He thanked me for the shout-out, and asked if I wanted to go backstage. Of course I did. Back there, Tommy shook my hand, and we talked for a while. I told him I'd seen him on the Run Now tour in St. Louis a decade or so before. "Oh, yeah," he said. "You danced." We had a good laugh about it.

We remained friendly in the years that followed, and I never missed a chance to see him live. And when fans would approach him, he remained as accessible as he'd been to me. Even when they'd tell him to his face that he should have been a bigger deal. *You should have a huge career! What happened?* If it is unpleasant, after a sweaty rock show, to hear that you were supposed to have been more successful than you've ended up being, which I would imagine that it is, you would not have known it to see him respond so graciously. Again and again.

My boyfriend and I caught him for what would be the last time a couple of months before his death, opening for Matthew Sweet at the Echo in Los Angeles. He crushed. A vicious guitar player, voice as strong as ever, looking far younger than a guy who was pushing sixty. Pegged jeans, as always. The crowd—there were more of us pushed up against the stage this time—sang every word of "Places That Are Gone" along with him. And then he got off stage and milled through the crowd, and people asked him why he wasn't bigger.

A great artist can make you feel like he's speaking directly to you. That's how Tommy Keene made me feel, and at the end of the day—and it is the end of the day—it doesn't matter whether ten or ten million other people had that same feeling. What matters is that we did.

Dave Holmes *is an editor-at-large for* Esquire Magazine, *and the author of the memoir* Party of One. *He's a television personality and a DJ for SiriusXM's* The Spectrum.

Joining a Fan Club: How Power Pop Outsiders Jellyfish Changed the Game

By Annie Zaleski

O N OCTOBER 25, 1990, during Jellyfish's show at the Roxy in Los Angles, a classic rock karaoke contest broke out onstage. More specifically, the quartet—then comprising drummer/ vocalist Andy Sturmer, guitarist Jason Falkner, keyboardist Roger Manning Jr., and his brother, bassist Chris Manning—started riffing on Styx's "Come Sail Away." "We're having a contest to see who sounds the most like Dennis DeYoung," a band member quips, as the song's pirouetting piano chords unfurl around him. After a strong start, the performance falters briefly, as the person who had been belting out lyrics with dramatic gusto runs out of steam. Someone else immediately picks up the slack, however, and the impromptu take on "Come Sail Away" glides toward a big finish: a slightly off-key, surging pre-chorus that explodes into drum splatters and finishes with the exuberant chorus.

For Jellyfish, this sort of vamping on other people's music wasn't out of the ordinary. In fact, covers were setlist staples, thanks in no small part to the San Francisco group's vast internal pop Rolodex, and Manning Jr.'s ability to perform random tunes on the fly. During concerts, this might translate to an improvised interlude with bits of Pilot's dewy seventies pop hit "Magic" that segued into Randy Newman's irreverent "Short People"—a pairing that actually happened during another 1990 performance—or Jellyfish unleashing more realized takes on Olivia Newton-John's "Have You Never Been Mellow?" and Wings' "Jet."

However, the group emphasized their covers aptitude on a much more prominent stage during a 1991 appearance on MTV's annual spring break sojourn to the beach. Back then, the channel's forays into seasonal fare were notorious for their incongruous musical bookings. (Radiohead-circa-*Pablo Honey*, whose members collectively looked glum, pale, and vampire-like, memorably set up shop by a pool one summer and cranked out grungy hits.) Jellyfish wasn't necessarily that out of place: the band had an arsenal of bouncy hits, including "Baby's Coming Back," that were perfect entertainment for a restless, party-hearty college crowd looking to let off steam.

Still, the MTV spring break gig was more notable for Jellyfish's interstitial interludes: a bevy of earnest classic rock covers that included Foreigner's "Double Vision," Chicago's "Saturday In the Park," David Bowie's "Jean Genie," Supertramp's "Logical Song," and Kansas' "Dust In the Wind." Jellyfish was clearly having a ball while blasting through their jukebox of hits, although crowd reactions were mixed. Some audience members clapped, spurred on by a desire to be on TV and/or overenthusiastic handlers; others simply stood around like statues.

Taking this MTV appearance at face value, Jellyfish looked like misfits, or at least the weird, artsy kids doing their thing while the popular crowd partied hard around them. Yet this performance highlighted the innate musical contradictions that simmered within the band. Jellyfish was the ultimate power pop outsiders—a band who appreciated, but largely eschewed, the British Invasion and Byrdsian signifiers favored by many groups, in favor of a singular, kaleidoscopic sound informed by seventies classic rock, psychedelic pop, and whiffs of glam and prog. However, this approach also made Jellyfish a mainstream music outsider, albeit one who embraced insider gestures—straightforward FM radio sounds, MTV appearances, major tour opening slots—while merrily subverting both expectations and trends.

Some of these subversions were low-key. For example, in 1992, Manning Jr. and Sturmer went incognito at the MTV Movie Awards. The duo provided irreverent, smoky-jazz-club percussion backup for actor William Shatner, who was doing his best impression of a slam poet while introducing the Best Song from a Movie nominees. The musicians were shrouded in darkness and wore identity-obscuring outfits, which further gave the skit an air of total absurdity.

Other subversions were much more obvious. After all, Sturmer was a drummer-singer who performed while standing up, bashing away on a no-nonsense kit at the front of the stage amid his bandmates. "Playing standing up is like trying to spin five plates in the air," he told *Modern Drummer* in 1993. "Playing drums standing up, singing, and talking to the audience is hard—but like anything else, you get used to it."

On occasion—such as during a 1991 appearance on *Late Night with David Letterman* featuring a chaotic, super-fast version of "All I Want Is Everything"—Sturmer's presence nudged the group's tempo forward in a helter-skelter skid. Yet, for the most part, his position inverted the balance of the band by bringing the rhythmic center to the forefront. This made drums less of a propulsive driving force and more an egalitarian part of Jellyfish's sound—a steadying presence.

The band's aesthetic vibe also inverted conventions. As noted in *Brighter Day: A Jellyfish Story*, Manning Jr. "had imagined the whole band experience to be a synthesis of favorite childhood associations: 10cc, *H.R. Pufnstuf*, bell bottoms, Henry Mancini, Gilligan's Island, Technicolor lunchboxes, the Sweet, Mego action figures, Filmation cartoons, and countless other influences." These are ambitious inspirations although, in practice, the pop culture ephemera and detritus came across as almost caricature-like. In press photos and onstage, the members of Jellyfish wore loud print pants, Dr. Seuss-esque striped hats, and snappy suit jackets in a rainbow of colors and textures. The cover of 1990's *Bellybutton* also resembles a fractured take on *Alice in Wonderland*: Each musician cavorts on and near the torso of a woman covered in frosting-like designs that were actually sculpted out of toothpaste.

During the early nineties, Jellyfish was far from the only act to dabble in such colorful looks: Poppy hair metal band Enuff Z'Nuff, dance mavens Dee-Lite, and party-punk giants the B-52s also created their own nostalgic psychedelic fantasies, and late-eighties rave culture fashion was also over the top. However, Jellyfish's look in particular felt like retro cosplay—a super-sized idea of kitsch, executed with a jubilant wink and earnest intentions. "This band has always enjoyed presenting itself colorfully," Manning Jr. told the *Los Angeles Times* in 1990. "A lot of that stuff we wear day in and day out. We just raided a lot of thrift stores."

Yet their playful, silly veneer didn't overshadow or undermine Jellyfish's immense musical gifts. Sturmer grew up a big jazz fan, particularly Miles Davis, Elvin Jones, and Art Blakey, and idolized prolific session stickmen such as Hal Blaine and Jim Keltner. Conversely, he learned to sing from listening to his older brother's Journey, Foreigner, and Bad Company albums. Being a frontman wasn't necessarily his main ambition, he admitted to *The St. Petersburg Times* in 1993: "I only started to sing because

I really felt like I wanted to start writing music, and there were no singers around. Actually, my singing just started as a really bad Sting impression because I was really into the Police. I remember my mom saying, 'Andy, just stick to the drums and you'll be fine.'"

Sturmer's high school friend, Manning Jr., was another analytical performer and voracious music fan who devoured MTV during its most eclectic days and soaked up jazz, punk, new wave, pop, and rock. He was also a keyboard expert, which broadened the band's sonic palette. Other band members brought similar depth and acumen: For example, Jason Falkner came to Jellyfish after a stint in Paisley Underground pop aficionados the Three O'Clock.

Together Sturmer and Manning Jr. harnessed their encyclopedic knowledge and years of friendship to craft songs that felt at once familiar and otherworldly. Jellyfish's music defied categorization, and prized complexity. Anyone looking for power pop's usual formula was out of luck: the band's take on the genre was luxurious and ornate, pristine and studied, and constructed out of elements culled from sixties and seventies pop and classic rock. Both 1990's *Bellybutton* and 1993's *Spilt Milk* felt like gilded FM radio flashbacks, full of songs that shone like polished jewels. Jellyfish elevated power pop to fine art much in the way Andy Warhol transformed pop art and advertising into luxe finery.

Sturmer's background in particular made his approach to music irreverent and unique. "I once read an interview with Carlos Santana, in which he said something that I think is really true," he told *Modern Drummer* in 1993. "He said that drummers write the prettiest melodies, because they aren't trained on a melodic instrument. When you're trained on a melodic instrument, you become so focused on the melodies that you work with that you can't see the most basic, beautiful, in-your-face melody. Coming from a drumming background, I go for the really obvious, pretty melody."

Where Jellyfish is concerned, obvious melodies aren't a synonym for banal or generic melodies. On the band's most complicated compositions, easy-to-grasp melodic throughlines provide grounding anchors for the music; on relatively straightforward tunes such as "I Wanna Stay Home," simpler melodies nudge lyrical beauty and emotional ache to the forefront. Sturmer was also adept at capturing a continuum of moods. The harmony-heavy chorus of "The Glutton of Sympathy" cascades gently, like a sled gliding downhill, while the vocals on "All I Want Is Everything" are as herky-jerky as a careening roller coaster.

Both of Jellyfish's studio albums cover a lot of sonic ground as well, beginning, of course, with the Beatles (especially the pop bacchanalia of *Sgt. Pepper's Lonely Hearts Club Band*) and the quirkier solo material of Ringo Starr and Paul McCartney/Wings. With this colorful foundation, Jellyfish piled on inspiration from Brian Wilson's askew pop perspectives; the meticulous, harmony-stacked FM rock favored by ELO, Supertramp, and Styx; lacquered glam flamboyance; and the seventies one-hit wonders that poured from the airwaves on the Casey Kasem American Top 40 countdown. Sturmer combined keening soul tone and rock and roll grit with a sighing falsetto—a rock and roll ringleader of a sonic fantasy full of glitter-stomp guitars and a rainbow-hued palette of keyboards.

Yet Jellyfish noticeably avoided the typical power pop signifiers—melancholy jangle, taut arrangements, solipsistic lyrics—in favor of denser textures and arrangements that unfurled like wicked tessellations. "The Man I Used to Be" unspools into topsy-turvy soul; "He's My Best Friend" was described by Manning Jr. in the *Spilt Milk* 2015 deluxe reissue liner notes as the band's "big thank you to Harry Nilsson for all the wonderful music he's given us"; "Bedspring Kiss" is jazzy, tropical bossa nova; and "Hush" nodded to the Beach Boys' barber pole-spun a cappella harmonies. *Spilt Milk*'s finale, "Brighter Day," even boasts a carnival orchestra full of brass, and jagged-lightning riffs that waver between sounding like Queen and Wings.

Both *Bellybutton* and *Spilt Milk* were coproduced by Albhy Galuten, who co-helmed several of the Bee Gees' *Saturday Night Fever* smashes (including "How Deep Is Your Love," "Stayin' Alive," "More Than a Woman," and "Night Fever") as well as the Dolly Parton and Kenny Rogers hit "Islands in the Stream." In other words, Galuten knew how to massage harmonies and guide ferocious talents into the pop stratosphere. In Jellyfish's case, this illuminated Sturmer's observational lyrics, throughout which personal truths are cloaked in metaphor, cleverness, and rich character sketches.

"Lyrically, I have a very short attention span," Sturmer once told *St. Petersburg Times*. "I see different puns developing and things, and I start going off in different tangents.... You get the face value of the lyrics, plus you get the secret decoder message and the pun side. So it's just more bang for your buck."

His ribald sense of humor cropped up on *Bellybutton*'s deceptively jaunty "Now She Knows She's Wrong." As harpsichord, synths, and twinkling percussion strut forward like an overconfident marching band, Sturmer sings about a woman discovering, twenty years after the fact, that her late partner wasn't exactly faithful: "Makin' love under the podium at the PTA / He's the principal of principles, this love gone bad." The lyricist played up such winking wordplay even more elsewhere in the song, specifically on the lines "He juggled his honesty / With two balls and an alibi." The latter phrase is delivered via multi-part harmony sung in a pretty falsetto, which adds a layer of sly humor that deliberately obscures the sentiment's risqué nature.

Yet Sturmer was also a genius at subtlety, particularly where character sketches were concerned. The bad boy narrator of "Baby's Coming Back" is sheepish about his inability to stay out of trouble, while "All I Want Is Everything" satirizes the unearned self-confidence intrinsic to those born into privilege. And *Bellybutton*'s opening track, "The Man I Used to Be," is a stunning song focused on a splintered family, starring a distant father who laments feeling far removed from his son's life.

"The Man I Used to Be" certainly set the mood on *Bellybutton*, through which a striking undercurrent of loneliness ripples. The protagonist of "She Still Loves Him" suffers in a relationship that's neglectful, and bordering on abusive; the main figure of "I Wanna Stay Home" honors a loving and cozy coupling but is weighed down by the idea that this idyllic time won't last forever; and the guilt-stricken narrator of "That Is Why" talks himself into (or is it out of?) confessing infidelity.

Sturmer's love of wordplay also shone throughout *Spilt Milk*, which boasted sophisticated and vibrant lyrics that read like elegant psychedelic poetry. The Shel Silverstein-esque "Sebrina Paste and Plato" pairs fanciful and fractured imagery ("I live to smell her tulips talk") with sing-songy rhythms and even a punny joke about "eating paste and Play-Doh," while "He's My Best Friend" is one of the more lighthearted songs ever penned about masturbation. On a more serious note, "The Glutton of Sympathy" drips with rich, velvety imagery that captures the ache of deep emotional anguish.

If Sturmer's *Bellybutton* protagonists only revealed glimpses of below-surface darkness, the characters scattered throughout *Spilt Milk* thrust storminess to the forefront. At times, the source of this is obliquely self-referential—"Joining a Fan Club" and "The Ghost at Number One" provide irreverent commentary on the bleak side of fame and rockstardom—although other songs hint at fissuring friendships and relationships. However, Sturmer's lyrics on *Spilt Milk* scan like more sophisticated renderings of his *Bellybutton* words.

Take "All Is Forgiven," which features a male figure with hidden vices, similar to the main character of "Now She Knows She's Wrong." Instead of relying on light humor, Sturmer this time around reaches for pointed religious imagery to illustrate the man's hypocrisy and lack of piety: "He tries to hide the cross he bears but splinters, like the truth, have always risen." The enduring impact of infidelity also drives "New Mistake," which hints at other Biblical moments, this time the original sin of Adam and Eve: "The baby had grown up and married a pop singer / I guess it was her turn to make her first mistake." Yet the album also offered a diverse range of emotions. The final track, "Brighter Day," provides a fitting punctuation mark on Jellyfish's proper studio album work, as it toes the line between cynicism and innocence, but ends on a cautiously optimistic note: "It can't help but be a brighter day."

For a brief, shining few years in the early nineties, Jellyfish enjoyed the spotlight thanks to tours with the Black Crowes, World Party, and Tears for Fears, and encounters with their heroes. Most notably, Sturmer and Manning Jr. cowrote and contributed harmonies to "I Don't Believe You," a bright-eyed song from Ringo Starr's 1992 album *Time Takes Time*. Along with fellow melodic iconoclasts Material Issue and the grungier Posies, Jellyfish even became part of the mainstream alternative rock conversation. In that sense, the band's biggest subversion of all was actually finding a way to fit in despite their stubborn quirks—while pushing power pop firmly into the modern age.

Annie Zaleski *is a Cleveland-based writer who's penned liner notes for the deluxe edition of R.E.M.'s* Out of Time *and is the author of the forthcoming* Why the B-52s Matter *and a 33 1/3 book on Duran Duran's* Rio.

Parallels: Sloan and Me

By Paul Myers

L ET ME START BY admitting that Sloan is one of only a handful of
power pop contemporaries whose band I would have jumped
ship from my own to join. I had a great time in my thing, Toronto
indie pop band the Gravelberrys (that's how we spelled it), but
there were times when I'd hear or see another band and think,
"Damn, they've cracked it." During the run of the Gravelberrys,
there were precisely three other bands in Canada that I would
have gladly chucked it in to join, as silly as that sounds now.
Toronto-based Edmonton expatriates the Pursuit of Happiness,
Vancouver's Odds, and finally Sloan, who had migrated to
Toronto from Halifax, Nova Scotia.

In the late 1980s, I took a day job as a clerk at a musical
copyright agency in Toronto, a perfect perch for a songwriter
and musician seeking to learn how the sausage was made in the
real music business. Our boss encouraged us to read all the trade
magazines and familiarize ourselves with the songs on the radio.
We all worked in one big open-plan room with a centrally located
stereo receiver and two speakers set far apart. My like-minded
work pals, Kevin and Ken, lobbied hard to keep it locked on
CFNY, the best alternative radio station in the city. If you grew
up in the Toronto area in the late seventies, eighties, and early

nineties, CFNY was the great melting pot of new music from England to the USA, as well as the most cutting edge rock music from the indie scene in Toronto and the outer reaches of Canada. It was on their influential airwaves that, one day in 1992, we found ourselves distracted by the slash and drone eloquence of Sloan's first single, "Underwhelmed."

Besides possessing a gift for harmony and melody, Sloan appeared to have an ear for clever wordplay.

She was underwhelmed, if that's a word
I know it's not, 'cause I looked it up
That's one of those skills that I learned in my school
I was overwhelmed, and I'm sure of that one
'Cause I learned it back in grade school
When I was young
She said, "You is funny"
I said, "You are funny"
She said, "Thank you"
And I said, "Nevermind"
She rolled her eyes
Her beautiful eyes.

In those early days of the internet, it was harder to get the band's backstory, so we cocked our ears to listen and see if the DJ had any background on these brash young men from the Maritimes. Over the coming weeks, we learned that Sloan had emerged from what was known as "the Halifax Pop Explosion," a kind of Canadian cousin to Seattle's so-called "Grunge" scene. Many of the other Pop Explosion bands, like Jale, Eric's Trip, and the Super Friendz, were also in fairly regular rotation on CFNY. There was a decidedly power pop attitude to a lot of bands of this era, and if you were me, you were secretly hoping acts like Jellyfish and the Posies were tipping the scales of indie rock toward a new power pop revolution, swinging the post-grunge pendulum way over to the post-Badfinger mindset of my own band. Indeed, a year later, CFNY would be playing our own indie power pop single, "Wonder Where You Are Tonight," which really upped my status around the office.

By then, Sloan was really taking off, and each successive single revealed them as some kind of *Haligonian* indie rock version of the Brill Building hit factory. I soon discovered that much of their eclecticism stemmed from the fact that all the songs were written by everyone in the band, and bassist Chris Murphy, guitarist Patrick Pentland, drummer Andrew Scott, and guitarist Jay Ferguson, mostly wrote on their own, changing lead vocalists, and sometimes instruments, depending on who wrote what. So in addition to Murphy's "Underwhelmed," I was also a fan of Pentland's "Sugartune," Scott's "500 Up," and Ferguson's "Lemonzinger."

Over their next few albums, *Twice Removed, One Chord to Another,* and *Navy Blues,* they evolved away from the slacker chic of "Underwhelmed," and began flexing their power pop muscles on singles like "Coax Me," "People of the Sky," and "The Lines You Amend," even adding such studio flourishes as crowd sound effects on "The Good In Everyone," and trumpets on "Everything You've Done Wrong."

Shortly after *Smeared,* I met Murphy at a party in Toronto where I basically fanboyed out on him all night. Despite this, we've been friends ever since. Today, I remain what might be called an "agnostic superfan," but I'm more convinced than ever that Sloan is the embodiment of the ideal power pop band: thundering rock guitars, catchy anthemic chorus melodies, glorious four-part harmonies, and a constant subtext of arrested adolescence, even well into their third decade as a band.

As we can see elsewhere in this anthology, the term power pop, like all genre labels, is frequently misunderstood or roundly rejected by some of the best progenitors in the field. I've personally read quotes from artists such as Marshall Crenshaw or Fountains of Wayne, who seemed a tad wary of being lumped in with a retro sound, and the so-called "skinny tie bands" playing for niche audiences at the International Pop Overthrow festival. While plenty of bands would kill for that chance, still others aspire to a broader reach for their music. So do the guys in Sloan consider themselves a power pop band? Well, it sort of depends on who you ask. Pentland always seems more metal-directed, Scott is an enigma, but the other two seem to enjoy being embraced by an audience that Murphy jokingly describes as "Beatles fans post Zeppelin and Sabbath latching onto bands doomed to commercial failure."

"Most of the originators of the genre were pretty great anyway," adds Murphy. "The Who, Cheap Trick, the Knack, I went crazy for 'My Sharona.' I like what I know about Big Star, the Raspberries, and Bad Company, although I never owned their records beyond hits collections. I would say pretty much all of my favorite bands could be described as power pop but I'm not sure if they are known as such. So, I'm fine for Sloan to be called power pop."

Like so many power pop success stories, Sloan initially got their foot in the door thanks to a major label misidentifying their sound. Just as the sixties and seventies saw the major labels scrambling to find the "Next Beatles" or the "New Bob Dylan," Sloan found themselves headhunted by Geffen at the height of the 1991 grunge wars, when every label was looking for the "Next Nirvana." Never mind that Halifax was as far from Seattle as a North American band could get. Never mind that, as a band, they had played little more than twelve shows. And never mind that, musically, the band had more in common with the Beatles, KISS, and Fleetwood Mac than their flannel-shirted contemporaries on Puget Sound.

Nevermind, indeed.

"Jay and I were KISS fanatics as little kids," says Murphy, "but we all watched music videos when they came on and taped them on our one or two precious VHS tapes. We all listened to CKDU, the college radio station in Halifax. Jay even had his own radio show. We all hung out at the Club Flamingo and played in local bands before Sloan. We all loved Nirvana and all of the things that led up to it and the shoe gazer scene in the UK. Our first album, *Smeared,* was a testament to that. But as we deviated from the sound of our first record, the differences in our musical tastes came out and were highlighted. I'm glad that we have four people capable of pulling us in different directions. It makes us harder to pin down and hopefully harder to get tired of."

The Geffen deal soon went away, along with Kurt Cobain and most of Sloan's contemporaries from the original Halifax Pop Explosion, but Sloan remained, retaining a healthy sense of arrested adolescence that belies an increasingly philosophical worldview as they've started to raise families of their own. They have also retained a uniquely Canadian sense of humor which, along with their shared Nova Scotia roots and age range, has kept Sloan's eight feet firmly on the ground.

"While we all loved Nirvana and the shoe gazer angst and seeming witlessness, we also loved SCTV," says Murphy. "When we were recording *Action Pact* in LA in 2003, we didn't go out to see other bands, but we did go out to see *comedy* at places like M Bar. It was great. All of the guys in our band have had a great sense of humor from the start, and we've been sharing jokes for decades now!"

As individuals, they've managed to retain their own identities within the collective by employing an every-man-for-himself approach to generating material; they rarely write or even play on each other's tracks anymore. According to Murphy, everyone in the band gets to essentially record and produce their own songs, in parallel, but share all the writing credits, profits, and royalties equally. The title of Sloan's ninth studio album, *Parallel Play*, was based on a term Murphy had heard used in child psychology.

"It's a term used to describe the lack of interaction between children aged one to three when they are playing side by side," Murphy told me. "It was an apt way to describe Sloan because some of us had young kids, but it's also the way we have worked from day one."

Jay Ferguson traces their free-for-all approach all the way back to their earliest days in Nova Scotia.

"We made our first album in a house with no aspiration to anything other than making our CD or our own cassette," says Ferguson. "And we signed to Geffen Records before we'd even played twenty shows on stage. But even on our earliest records, we were never a band that really got together in the room and jammed out a song."

When drummer and fine art painter Andrew Scott made the move to Toronto, the distance meant each member of Sloan began writing in more isolation. And even after the rest of the band joined him in the city, that individualism stuck.

"As a result," Ferguson once told me, "I think if anybody in this band did a solo album, it wouldn't sound very much different than Sloan, we're a bit of four-headed monster that way."

That monster can be highly prolific, often heroically so, as on their twenty-two-song marathon double album, wryly entitled *Never Hear the End of It*. As individual as they are, Sloan seem to share a collective glee at just being in a band, and Ferguson admits to being a keen student of other people's bands and working arrangements.

"I always wanted to see how these bands did it," says Ferguson. "I think Chris and Patrick's aspirations were the same, although I think Andrew was into it more for fun, at first, he was studying to be a fine artist and I don't think he was imagining being in a band for a living when he was fifteen, you know?"

Sloan frequently ruminates about what it means to hold onto one's youthful exuberance while fighting the good fight as the old models of the music business crumble around them. Their parallel play dates have turned into a full-time job, a fact Murphy dwells on in his song "I'm Not A Kid Anymore."

Once upon a time, I was on the scene
An attitude and a jacket o' jean
These days I'm up to my ass in routine
Another day, another duller
I relied heavily on Styx and Stones
Not so much Styx once I heard the Ramones
I got a job, an anagram of loans
We work the other nine to five
I'm not a kid anymore.

It's a great example of Sloan wit, right down to the clever anagram of the band's name. But while Murphy takes the ludicrousness of rockism with a grain of salt, he and Pentland's "Money City Maniacs" brings more gravitas to the matter, declaring that "at the heart of the travelling band…there's a driving need to hit the yellow line."

The rest of the song fairly bristles with the spirit of stoic perseverance.

Hey you
You've been around for a while
If you admit that you were wrong, then we'll admit that we're right
Hey you
Come along for the ride
We'll hit the money city if it takes us all night.

In a band of solo artists, Pentland may be the most solitary Sloaner.

"Patrick works much more on his own, and he's much more insular," concedes Ferguson, who admits he sometimes doesn't know Pentland's songs on any given album until the band reconvenes to mix them all down. "He's very into his own style of sounds and things like that. It's just the way we work."

I've come to realize that sometimes the only thing gluing together Sloan's component parts is their sing-along choruses where all four of them come together to create their distinctive harmony. More than anything else, it's the way their voices blend, and their favored intervals, that truly define their sound.

"No matter who played the music on the backing tracks," says Ferguson, "our voices turn it into a Sloan song."

And somehow, this blend has made Sloan a model of everything I love in a power pop band, and Murphy says he'll gladly accept that label, citing so many of his most beloved bands, including GBV, Supergrass, Nirvana, Weezer, the Strokes, Bowie, Queen, and even glam acts such as the Sweet, as having strong traces of power pop in their DNA.

"Can they all be considered power pop too?" Murphy asks, rhetorically. "Why not? I guess I've heard it said that if you can be described as something else first, then you are not considered power pop."

In 2014, I collaborated with fellow guitarist and songwriter John Moremen under the group name the Paul & John to produce the album *Inner Sunset*. It was my first full album since the Gravelberrys released *Bowl of Globes* in 1993, and I found that I had learned a lot in the interim. We're both big XTC, Elvis Costello, and Beatles fans, and our name even winks at the famous Fabs, but it's not strictly a power pop record. While John is a fan of power pop, he's not as quick to identify with the label as I've been, but that's the nature, and the beauty, of collaboration, and I think I was more open to it thanks to my knowledge of Sloan's collective approach. We really like our music, and I love that it's the combination of our tastes that defines it. It's our music, and significantly, it's not Sloan's music, because I've also come to realize that it's better to let Sloan be Sloan, and I'll just do what I do over here. No one else needs to be Sloan.

And besides, even the four solo artists that make up that four-headed monster have worked really hard just to be Sloan, so why would anyone else even try?

But hey, like the song says, if it feels good, do it.

Paul Myers *is a Toronto, Canada-born and Berkeley, California-based writer and musician who has written for* Mojo, MIX, Crawdaddy, *and* Fast Company, *and is the author of four books, including* A Wizard a True Star: Todd Rundgren in the Studio *and most recently* Kids in the Hall: One Dumb Guy, *in 2018. His short autobiographical piece,* The Cherokee Record Club, *appeared in Rare Bird's 2013 prog rock anthology,* Yes Is The Answer.

You Can Only Be Free:
The Unknowable Robert Pollard's
Unbreakable Bond with Power Pop

By Dylan Champion

POWER POP IS A ghost. Behind its joy, energy, and sugar-to-the vein hooks, it's a genre based on the memory of something beloved that is no more. It's music made by record collectors who ran out of records and decided to make more themselves.

So what about this defiantly genius, unlikely, largely uncategorizable outfit from Dayton Ohio called Guided By Voices? Are they—and their avuncular wizard/captain Bob Pollard—power pop? Surely GBV is no one's quintessential power pop band, and yet, start looking GBV right in their enigma-spun eyes and you find yourself on a deep dive into the soul of the genre.

For the sake of a starting place, let's posit that, in the loosest terms, power pop is music made starting in the 1970s, inspired by 1950s doo-wop and rock and roll and more so sixties surf, pop, and British Invasion—embodied most quintessentially in the work of the Beatles prior to *Sgt. Pepper's*. This is the music power poppers seek to conjure and reanimate in a more electric, rhythmically throttling incarnation. Broadly termed—it's bubble gum with balls.

So are GBV such conjurers? Even if you've only just communed a bit with their seminal trilogy—*Propeller*, *Bee Thousand*, and *Alien Lanes*—you know how deeply they are engaged in such reanimation: the Motown-cum-Merseyside beat variations, the ballsy power chords with cascadingly catchy lead lines chiming atop, the Anglophilic earworm melodies draped in harmonies and theatrically delivered in Pollard's Lennon-of-Dayton lilt. And the hooks—oh, baby, the hooks—all packed in tight, short, sugar-concentrating songs. From early classics like "Quality of Armor" (*Propeller*) or "My Valuable Hunting Knife" (*Alien Lanes*)—both of which point lo-fi pinhole cameras into the musical heart of power pop—to full-studio, mid-career faves like "Glad Girls" (*Isolation Drills)* or "Teenage FBI" (*Do The Collapse*), GBV's relationship with the genre is irrefutable. Pollard goes where he wishes musically, from garage to post punk to psychedelia, but through over 100 albums and more than 2,000 songs—an output that defies precedent—his power pop tendencies are so ubiquitous and crucial to his oeuvre as to make an even stronger empirical case for his belonging to that world. Upon the 2018 release of *Space Gun*, Sean O'Neal and Katie Rife of avclub.com noted that, fundamentally, GBV "rarely breaks the two-minute mark—three minutes would be edging toward proggy self-indulgence—in its sharp, jagged nuggets of British Invasion-indebted power pop and shambolic garage rock."

Fair enough, but this music isn't normal. GBV doesn't just fit in. They barely belong under the much larger, sheltering thrift store umbrella of "indie music." Yes, they're now elder statesmen of that scene, but more because no one knew where else to put them than because they belong. Pollard's genius is rooted in both his contradictory nature and his trenchant, irascible ill ease with belonging. He's an artist/poet who'd rather eat pizza and drink pitchers of Bud Light after a sweat-drenched pick-up basketball game than ruminate on the societal injustices or anti-corporate ethos so central to the indie scene. He's nobody's hipster—he's got a history of brawling with even his best pals and is the proud founder of an Elks Lodge-style man cave called "The Monuments Club," which is both a home for professional drinking and an incubator for his creation. And look, I'm pretty sure Thurston Moore can throw a ball, but Pollard is a full-on jock—a star pitcher and quarterback through college. And while he's traveled the world, he still prefers Dayton, thank you very much, and a pitcher of the lite American stuff.

Musically, his cock rock proclivities dangle dangerously outside the smug, anti-rock star orthodoxy of the indie music scene. He high kicks because it's fucking cool, not because it's ironic. Pavement's Stephen Malkmus languidly snarks, "Stone Temple Pilots, they're elegant bachelors. Foxy to me, are they foxy to you?" on the iconic classic "Range Life," while on "See My Field" (from 2018's *Space Gun*) Pollard grandiosely commands, "Go on, be a spectator. See my field. I discovered lightning in a jar!"

It's not that he's got a copy of *Purple* in his cassette deck, it's that he wants to rock, and he wants to rock right. This earnest belief in rock's supreme power, the unabashed love for the stuff, the show, the high-kicking without irony—actually somewhat ironically—brings Pollard even more into harmony with power pop because, unlike the larger indie scene where it's housed, power pop ain't about irony. It's about genuine reverence—pure, formative love for a music that channels the chaotic, aching energy of, heretofore at least, adolescent boys. As has been said, it's music made by record collecting obsessives—okay, nerds—who, having worn out all the records that sounded good, had to make more themselves. Pollard makes this exact point himself in a 1999 interview with

Jeff Stratton of *The Onion*: "There are some good underground bands...like Superchunk, Pavement, Sebadoh, and the Grifters... But if you look for good new music, it's just not there... So I'm always looking for old sixties and seventies compilations. If you're looking for a particular type of song that's not around or that doesn't exist anymore, the only thing you can really do is try to write it yourself."

His desire to make more of a music that's gone is fundamental to power pop.

Pollard is of a different age. Born in 1957, he didn't emerge from his cave of artistic obscurity until well into his thirties with 1992's *Propeller*. Never before had an artist of this stature only just begun *emerging* from near total anonymity at thirty-five. He saw the Beatles appear on Ed Sullivan in 1964—*when it happened*—at the age of seven. He was imprinted early, in those tender years of youth, with the Beatles performing "All My Lovin'," "Till There Was You," and "She Loves You"—a holy trinity to power pop's genesis. Ever since that show, he's obsessively collected vinyl. As a fourth grader, he would skip lunch, eat packets of mustard to slake hunger, and spend the money instead on 45s, according to Matthew Cutter's 2018 biography *The Closer You Are*. When he couldn't afford a record, or he'd bought all there were, he trained his obsession on crafting his own made-up album covers, complete with fictional band names, song titles, lyrics, and liner notes. According to Cutter, "some folded out like triple albums, others were concept albums, a few had stories written in them." By the end of high school, he'd made nearly a hundred, which he later destroyed for fear he'd be "revealed as some kind of lunatic," which, he avers, "I was."

This obsession with *image*—the package that visually drives the magic illusion of the music—is another deep tie between

Pollard and power pop. Pop art is an inextricable part of the genre, from Warhol to Roy Lichtenstein, whose comic book style is the virtual logo for power pop, imitated on hundreds of compilations, posters, and flyers. Pollard was making album covers in a pop art collage style before he knew a single guitar chord. Had he never written a song, his visual art, which he shows now in galleries (see robertpollardart.com), would make him both worthy of acclaim and at least a welcome guest to the club.

But being a collagist doesn't make you power pop any more than having a serious vinyl habit does. To *be* power pop, you need the drive and skill to *reincarnate* music from that aforementioned period. The fifties through *Sgt. Pepper's* is supernatural not because it's the *birth* of rock and roll, but because it's the moment when pop and rock first took the globally transcendent form it would maintain. The numbers have been outstripped, and there are more historically significant moments, but no period was as transformative, revolutionary, or complete in popular music. That's why this era has remained so influential for artists born in the decades following. Kids today are still weaned on Beatles records for a good reason. This was the biblical time for popular music (thus the zealous debates over respective readings of the holy texts). The energy of this period was so great that—to mash metaphors—it was a musical big bang, itself quickly overtaken by the many new planets and galaxies it spawned, leaving a comparatively small record of its own existence and a greater thirst for more than any other single moment in popular music.

That magnetic draw is power pop's creative engine. For Pollard, ever since watching those four fellas from England flickering like apparitions on a black and white TV in 1964, he sang and wrote music compulsively until—absurdly—nearly three decades later,

Propeller finally drew its own light to his shadowy legerdemain. Per Cutter's book, another reviewer said at the time of *Propeller's* release simply, "Living in the past? This could be your modern-day bread and butter."

The conjuring was working.

Pollard binds himself closer to power pop by repeatedly citing the Who—another band whose early work is deeply intertwined with the genre—as a key influence. He calls their iconic record *Who's Next* not merely his favorite record, but his blueprint for it all. "[It's] my favorite album of all time," he says in *Spin* in 2004. "The Who was totally my model."

So cool, the smoking gun! After all, Pete Townshend *coined the term "power pop."* GBV *are* a power pop band! Yeah, but like Columbo turning around with his glass eye and long-ashed cigar stub, there's just one more thing…a few more, actually. About Mr. Townshend, for example, there's a problem. *Who's Next* came out in 1971 and is *not* a power pop record, but the moment when the Who at last abandoned their Beatles-wannabe beginnings to fully become a thunderous, swaggering arena rock band. Townshend coined the term "power pop" to describe the band's 1967 single "Pictures of Lily," four eternally long musical years before *Who's Next* (in the hazy black and white video for "Lily," the soon-to-be bare-chested Roger Daltrey is ill at ease, bridling for freedom from his white matching Beatles jacket while Moon and a jacketless Townshend seem to have already left the station). "Lily" is absolutely a power pop prototype—in 1995, Teenage Fanclub released their creamily catchy power pop single "Sparky's Dream," which basically lifts whole the chorus of "Pictures of Lily." But by 1971, the Who were "Baba O'Riley"—screaming vocals; massive arena power chords and drums; bluesy guitar leads; apocalyptic lyrics; and a fragmented, psychedelic arrangement. This is not power pop. By '71, the Who had only slightly less to do with power pop than Black Sabbath.

So Pollard begins to slip, like so much smoke, through power pop's clutches. Here, perhaps, Columbo's glass eye turns upon us with a final, damning fact. Despite his age, his fanatical record collecting, his pop art gifts, and his incomparably prolific output of perfectly power pop musical compositions, Pollard's lyrics are rarely—really never—power pop.

Maybe power pop's most crucial trait is its simplest—the songs are about girls. Duh, the genre is entirely propelled by the lustful yearnings of (heretofore) teenage boys. For sex, yes, but for more—identity, love, and meaning in their simplest, earliest forms. Take a granddaddy tune like 1972's "Go All The Way," by fellow Ohioans the Raspberries. The track is literally two separate song chunks smashed together in some sort of musical nuclear fusion to make an explosive new thing—the moment of the genre's birth. It's Eric Carmen putting chocolate and peanut butter together for the first time. There's the balls-out power chord hook—modern, wild, and distorted—juxtaposed with a honey-dripped, 1950's high school dance verse/chorus melody more reminiscent of the Drifters than even the Beatles. Lyrically, the song is a wooing, pubescent Jekyll and Hyde emancipation, with Carmen first sweetly crooning:

I never knew how complete love could be
Till she kissed me and said,
Baby, please, go all the way
It feels so right
Being with you here tonight

Then, back to the power guitars, and Carmen wails in full rock and roll rasp:

Before her love
I was cruel and mean
I had a hole in the place
Where my heart should have been

This *is* the power and the pop. That basic juxtaposition continued to evolve with songs like the Flamin' Groovies' 1976 masterpiece "Shake Some Action," which tapped even more into the pure lust of it all:

I will find a way
To get to you some day
Shake some action's what I need
To let me bust out at full speed

Then, in 1979, the number one hit "My Sharona" by the Knack is oft cited as the form's quintessence—a perfect marriage of beat, guitar hook, and earworm melody, though arguably, Doug Fieger's lyrics push things to a creepy edge: "Never gonna stop, give it up, such a dirty mind I always get it up, for the touch of the younger kind."

Power pop, much like Pollard, has never stopped producing, from the undervalued 1980 song "What I Like About You," by the Romantics, through the 1990s, when the indie scene was littered with adoring, at times masterful, power pop gems like Matthew Sweet's "Girlfriend" (1991) or Material Issue's "What Girls Want" (1992). It didn't stop at the turn of the aughts either, with OK Go and Jimmy Eat World churning out power pop hits all the way up to a "modern" example like 2012's "Heaven" by the Walkmen (yup, that's a power pop song). For nearly a half century now, power pop's ghost has remained, like a thing that can't die.

While Pollard is a master of the *musical* alchemy of power pop, for fifty years now, the genre has also never stopped talking about the adolescent yearning for girls—something Pollard's never really done.

If ever an album cover embodied his *lyrical* soul, it's GBV's greatest hits compilation *Human Amusements at Hourly Rates*, where he's literally dressed in wizard garb, face half shrouded in an over-large hood, like Emperor Palpatine from Star Wars relishing Luke's rage, but with eyes closed in a dream. Across the vast expanse of this output, his lyrics are mystical, abstract, questing— both defiantly cocksure and knowingly crestfallen—but never about getting or even wanting the girl. Marginal exceptions are scant and flawed, including "Your Name Is Wild" (a beautiful song about his daughter) and "Glad Girls," which actually spells out clearly his very non-power pop intentions:

Hey glad girls
I only wanna get you high...
With the sinking of the sun
I've come to greet you
Clean your hands and go to sleep
Confess the dreams
Of good and bad men all around
Some are lost
And some have found
The light that passes through me

On the jabbingly power poppy opus "My Valuable Hunting Knife," Pollard deliberately turns the archetype of songs-about-girls on its head by replacing the girl with an anthropomorphized hunting knife:

I want to start a new life
With my valuable hunting knife
She will shine like a new girl
And I want to shout out our love to the world (Hit it!)

Ultimately, the knife doesn't really cut it:

Everything I think about, I think about
Everything I talk about, I talk about with you
But you don't know what I go through
You don't know

His often brilliant lyrics, viewed in total, become less abstract in their primary focus: exploring the mythos and ethos of Bob Pollard as supernatural rock conjurer and his philosophy of living life freely through music. No time for girls when yer busy with the stuff of existential transfiguration—imbued with both a youthful thrust for freedom and the seasoned wisdom to know it's all an illusion.

To dine alone
To build a private zone
Or trigger a synapse
To free us from our traps

These lines, from the beloved favorite "The Official Ironman Rally Song" off *Under the Bushes Under the Stars*, are as central to Pollard as they are antithetical to power pop.

In the end, Uncle Bob eludes capture—avoiding membership in the club. Take the self-referential, encapsulating classic, "I Am a Scientist":

I am a scientist, I seek to understand me
I am an incurable and nothing else behaves like me

Maybe we should take his word for it.

Dylan Champion *is a songwriter, producer, journalist, and founder of the acclaimed indie rock band Shapes of Race Cars. His music has been featured in dozens of films, TV shows, and commercials worldwide. His writing has appeared in numerous outlets including* The Hollywood Reporter *and* wga.org, *and he is the author of* Script Tease, *a collection of interviews with iconic screenwriters.*

Power Pop for Slackers

By S. W. Lauden

*Hip-Hop, country music, and post-grunge squall can take
a partial summer vacation. I'm applying some #45 sunblock
and putting up a sign saying "gone fishing for power pop."*

—Ken Tucker, NPR Rock Critic

1996. A DRINKING BUDDY and I lived in El Segundo, California.
Our apartment was in the Bermuda Triangle between a sewage
treatment plant, oil refinery, and LAX. Jets rumbled by overhead
every eight minutes around the clock, causing the putrid air to
vibrate. We kept the beer flowing and the stereo cranked up in
response to our toxic environment. At least we lived at the beach.

The rock world was in a similar situation mid-decade, groping
for "the new Seattle" as the pendulum swung out of control. Record
company A&R teams were deployed from the coasts to scour the
country for "the next big thing." It was an exciting time in some
ways, with alternative rock clearing the way for pop punk, ska, and
Britpop, but the one hit wonders were piling up fast (think hooky
alt rock radio favorites like "Cannonball," "No Rain," and "Loser").
This stylistic pinballing left some music fans with whiplash, but it
was fertile ground for musicians who love high-energy pop rock
with catchy melodies and plenty of hooks. The major label door
was open a crack in the nineties and a few power pop acts snuck
through, often under the guise of other genres.

It was around this time that a quirky sugar bomb called Fountains of Wayne exploded in our El Segundo apartment. To say the song "Radiation Vibe" helped to shake me and my roommate from our post-grunge stupor would be an understatement. We listened to the band's self-titled debut album on repeat in an effort to dissect exactly what made the music seem so refreshing, eventually surrendering to the unknowable simplicity of pop rock gems like "Joe Rey," "She's Got a Problem," "Leave the Biker," and "Barbara H." I was hooked like a lot of rock critics at the time, many of whom filed Fountains Of Wayne under "power pop."

"Funny, because I sort of remember thinking the record we'd made was really 'rock' sounding compared to the stuff we did when we were younger, which didn't have any distorted guitars or barre chords," said Adam Schlesinger, bassist and half of Fountains of Wayne's songwriting duo with lead vocalist/guitarist Chris Collingwood.

In addition to Fountains of Wayne, Schlesinger is an accomplished songwriter who has also played with Ivy, Tinted Windows, and Fever High. His song "That Thing You Do," for the 1996 Tom Hanks movie of the same name, was nominated for an Academy Award and Golden Globe. He has also been nominated for a Tony Award and an Emmy for his stage and screen work. Dude's a songwriting machine.

"I think in the (music) industry, there's a general sense that the power pop label means 'bands that don't sell.' Although there was a brief period in the early-to-mid-nineties where some bands that might be fairly labeled power pop did sell," he added.

It's true that power pop persistently bubbled under throughout the nineties. Teenage Fanclub, Matthew Sweet, Material Issue, Redd Kross, and the Posies waved the flag in the first half of the decade. By the mid-nineties, bands like the Lemonheads, Sloan, and Weezer had successfully blended elements of power pop with alternative rock and grunge. Meanwhile, Britpop delivered an endless rush of pop thrills via Oasis, Blur, Elastica, Supergrass, Silver Sun, and countless others—stealthily avoiding the power pop label and its associated curse of collectible obscurity.

Given the variety of voices, influences, and career trajectories of so many end-of-century bands, opinions vary about what qualified as power pop in the nineties. By this point, the genre's golden age was pushing twenty and the small but dedicated legions dwindled. Fewer fans were able to speak knowledgably about the Records, Bram Tchaikovsky, Pezband, or even the Knack, but much of the old guard was still reluctant to let new members into their walled garden. At least not without a few purity tests. But that's the beautiful thing about power pop fandom—it's the debate club of rock and roll. It's not intended to be mean-spirited or malicious, but you better take it seriously or risk getting gutted in the record store aisles or on the killing floor of social media. And afterward we can all go have a drink and listen to some rare vinyl together.

Fountains of Wayne entered the fray in 1996 under the alternative rock banner, finding themselves in the skeptical gaze of this lost rock and roll tribe. Schlesinger was happy the band was embraced at all but never claimed to be a power pop expert.

"I just know what I liked growing up. Part of the thing with power pop is that there isn't this rigid set of rules like with certain subgenres of metal or punk where you're supposed to know what's cool and not cool."

What Schlesinger liked growing up—like countless musicians before him—was the Beatles. Gifted the band's albums by a cool aunt when he was still a toddler, Schlesinger built his lifelong love of music starting with *Meet The Beatles* (drawing himself into the band photo on the back). It took some time, but he eventually branched out during his formative years, studying jazz piano and taking classical piano lessons along the way. "I was listening to Broadway music and pop music from all different eras, but I already had the Beatles in my blood."

It's this Fab Four foundation that fuels much of the band's power pop tendencies. Fountains Of Wayne don't sound like the Beatles, and they are in no way revivalists, but it's hard to deny the influence. Although rarely worn on their sleeves, winks and nods to John, Paul, George, and Ringo—and other power pop gods like Brian Wilson of the Beach Boys or Ray Davies of the Kinks—are threaded throughout their six releases including five studio albums and the 2005 compilation, *Out-of-State Plates* (which opens with the Ken Tucker quote at the beginning of this essay). It's perhaps most pronounced on their more subdued tracks like "Sick Day" (*Fountains Of Wayne*), "Fire Island" (*Welcome Interstate Managers*), and "Places" (*Out-of-State Plates*).

"Hey Julie" (*Welcome Interstate Managers*) is notable in this context because it takes a formula firmly established by "A Hard Day's Night" and updates it for a jaded twenty-first century audience. Where the Beatles are "working like a dog" to "bring you money to buy you things," Fountains of Wayne have a more tongue-in-cheek take on coming home after a day in the cube farm:

> *Working all day for a mean little man*
> *With a clip-on-tie and a rub-on tan*
> *He's got me running 'round the office like a dog around a track*
> *But when I get home,*
> *You're always there to rub my back*

Those colorful turns of phrase, peppered with bleak comedic observations and use of oddly specific details, are hallmarks of the quartet's lyrics. And it's their distinctive lyrical style that probably fuels most arguments about whether or not they truly rate as power pop. This is because Fountains of Wayne eschews much of the earnestness and double-entendre innocence of their sixties forebears (and their seventies and eighties acolytes), instead bringing Generation X slacker-isms and a dash of irony (a power pop no-no according to many purists) to their hooky tunes. Thematically, many of their songs may tread familiar power pop ground (often about girls with names like "Maureen," "Yolanda Hayes," and "Denise"), but Schlesinger and Collingwood also tap their eighties suburban upbringings—New Jersey and Pennsylvania, respectively—to deliver off-beat tales about failed baseball careers, survival cars, laser shows, cordless phones, shopping malls, sex lawyers, and (of course) Hackensack.

"I don't think we ever set out to be snarky or poke fun at anything. I think it was more about trying to put our own stamp on things," Schlesinger said. "The hard thing when you're starting out as a musician is to figure out what your own musical identity is, especially if you're somebody who likes a lot of different kinds of music. You have to consciously pick a lane that feels like you and define yourself."

Schlesinger thinks that Fountains of Wayne was often successful in this regard but felt their songs about "our friends and things that we thought were funny or cool" sometimes led to misunderstandings about the band's intentions. Occasionally accused of looking down on the people they wrote about, Schlesinger says that he and Collingwood saw themselves as the sad sack characters they constructed mundane worlds around ("even if we weren't being sincere, it was never with any kind of malice toward anyone").

Their unique style and idiosyncratic lyrics continued to evolve over the course of the songwriting partnership. Inspired by Lennon and McCartney, Schlesinger and Collingwood shared credit for all Fountains of Wayne songs even though they rarely wrote together after the band's earliest days. Part of the partnership was purely pragmatic ("a way of avoiding fighting about money"), but mostly born of mutual respect, shared ambition, and a spirit of healthy competition.

"When Chris and I first started out in our teens and early twenties, we were writing stuff that was very imitative. Then we kind of disbanded for a few years, and when we got back together, Chris had written a couple of songs that felt qualitatively different," Schlesinger said. "I got really inspired by—and jealous of—his new songs, but it opened up this path where we could write about things that felt like our real selves."

Where Collingwood had a more fully developed storytelling style and innate sense of humor from the start, Schlesinger says he had to work at developing his voice for Fountains of Wayne. An epiphany came when he dove into songwriters like Randy Newman and Paul Simon who wrote from the perspective of unreliable narrators instead of making everything about the singer's literal worldview.

Add Newman and Simon to the eclectic list of influences that started with the Beatles, and you'd only be scratching the surface. Schlesinger says a lot of eighties music figured into their musical alchemy, including bands Collingwood turned him on to (Aztec Camera, Everything But The Girl, the Smiths, and the Cure) and bands he already liked (the Pretenders, the Police, and Elvis Costello & the Attractions). It's some of these eighties influences—along with nods to the Cars and Rick Springfield—that informed their biggest hit, "Stacy's Mom"; a song that inverts the lecherous theme of the Knack's "My Sharona" to focus on the forbidden feelings a horny teenage boy has for his friend's mom. You know, power pop!

"The band was an amalgamation of a lot of things we were into," Schlesinger said. "It was just our way of filtering a lot of the music we liked through our own personalities. We were really just trying to entertain each other."

When asked which of his songs he thinks are the most power pop, Schlesinger points to "It Must Be Summer" (*Utopia Parkway*) and "This Better Be Good" (*Traffic and Weather*). Both songs highlight Schlesinger's power pop prowess ("There have been certain songs where I just tried all the power pop tricks I knew"), with the previously mentioned catchy hooks and lyrical quirks on full display.

"This Better Be Good" starts off with a line about "holding hands" (with "yeah" and "baby" thrown into the Beach Boys-y chorus for good measure) before devolving into an accusatory diatribe about the object of his affection's Dockers-wearing beau who was spotted at the Gap. Meanwhile, "It Must Be Summer" opens with a brief Byrds-y guitar lick before giving way to a bouncy groove that underscores heartbreaking lyrics delivered with characteristic nonchalance:

It must be summer
'Cause the days are long
And I dial your number
But you're gone, gone, gone
I'd set out searching
But the car won't start
And it must be summer
'Cause I'm falling apart

"It Must Be Summer" and "This Better Be Good" are both great Fountains of Wayne songs, and are in many ways indicative of the band's overarching style—but neither were hits, so you'd be hard pressed to find many casual fans who could easily rattle them off if pressed for a list of favorites. Unfortunately, most people simply know them as "the 'Stacy's Mom' band."

In the end, that might be the most power pop thing about Fountains of Wayne. Unlike the sixties hit makers that inspired the genre, the majority of power pop's most revered acts live and die in relative obscurity. The lucky ones—like the Raspberries, the Knack, Dwight Twilley, the Romantics, and a handful of others—momentarily enjoy the mainstream spotlight before fading back into the shadows. It is in this later category that Fountains of Wayne seems to reside, at least by commercial standards. And Schlesinger is totally cool with that.

"For some reason 'Stacy's Mom' connected," he concludes. "We get put on a lot of 'One Hit Wonder' lists because of it, which is fine. I'm happy we were known for one song than for no songs."

S. W. Lauden *is the author of the Greg Salem punk rock PI series in-cluding* Bad Citizen Corporation, Grizzly Season *and* Hang Time. *His Tommy & Shayna novellas include* Crosswise *and* Crossed Bones. *A new novelette,* That'll Be The Day: A Power Pop Heist, *was released in June 2019. S. W. Lauden is the pen name of Steve Coulter, drummer for Tsar and The Brothers Steve.*

More info at http://swlauden.com.

From Blown Speakers: The Brainy Power Pop of Allan Carl Newman

By Chris Holm

IN HIS OPINION ON 1964's *Jacobellis v. Ohio*, Supreme Court Justice Potter Stewart famously described pornography as follows: "I shall not today attempt further to define the kinds of material I understand to be embraced within that shorthand description; and perhaps I could never succeed in intelligibly doing so. But I know it when I see it."

Power pop is much the same; strip away the superficial trappings, and your ears will always lead you true.

Take the album in your hands, for example. A debut, you're told. The cover—a kitschy folk art image of a naked man and woman, uh…kissing horizontally while a rather Freudian ram looks on—is at once smarmy and obtuse. Ditto the band's name, the New Pornographers, and the album's title, *Mass Romantic*, both of which are rendered in vaguely flesh-toned gothic letters against a red matte. And oh, yeah, the whole thing's surrounded by a mock wood frame.

What, exactly, are they going for here?

The press release isn't much help. The label, Mint Records, is an obscure Canadian outfit whose releases number in the low forties. They claim the band's a super group, but the members' names mean nothing to you. Who are these guys? What kind of music do they play? Twee indie folk? Oversexed alt-rock? Ironic white-kid funk?

You place the record on the platter and drop the needle.

The drummer counts off. The title track begins. Guitar and keys blast out of the gate, the former a propulsive rhythm, the latter a simple melody. The rest of the band follows close behind. Then the singer—one of three, you'll later realize—launches into the first verse like a woman with something to prove. By the time the chorus kicks in, Beach Boys harmonies swirling dizzily around a soaring lead vocal, you're grinning like an idiot.

This, my friends, is power pop...isn't it?

"I never thought of us as a power pop band," Carl Newman, the driving force and principal songwriter behind the New Pornographers, told *Magnet Magazine* in 2017. "I always thought we were definitely an indie rock band. We were trying to do pop, but pop music that's a little off. It seemed to me at the time that there were bands that were fun party bands, but they were lightweight. They didn't have very good songs; they were just a party band. Then there were the bands that were the respected, good bands, and they seemed like not much fun at all. I thought, 'Why don't we try to merge these things?'"

Merge them they did, and the result—wherever you choose to shelve it—is forty-odd minutes of ebullient rock bliss. As a twenty-something who'd aged out of the hardcore punk of my youth but felt out of place among a sea of stone-faced indie fans who favored nodding imperceptibly to dancing, hearing Newman and company for the first time was nothing short of a revelation.

In 2000, when *Mass Romantic* was released, dubbing the New Pornographers a super group was likely some combination of snark, hubris, and savvy marketing. It was true that Newman had fronted two prior bands, but neither had developed much of a following. Dan Bejar's idiosyncratic art rock project, Destroyer, was little known outside of Vancouver's music scene. Neko Case, whose vocal talents led off the record, had arguably made the biggest splash of the three. She had released two well-received alt-country albums—both of which Newman played on—but her critical and commercial breakthrough was still years away.

Looking back, however, the moniker was prophetic.

Mass Romantic was met with rapturous reviews, garnering comparisons to the Beach Boys, the Beatles, Big Star, the Buzzcocks, Cheap Trick, Robyn Hitchcock, Roxy Music, and T. Rex, to name but a few. It wound up seventeenth on the Village Voice's influential Pazz & Jop critics' poll, won Canada's Juno Award for Alternative Album of the Year, and landed them a Friday night showcase at 2001's South by Southwest, where they were joined onstage by Ray Davies.

Suddenly—in music-geek circles, at least—the New Pornographers were inescapable.

"It didn't just explode out of nowhere," Newman later said of *Mass Romantic*. "It was very sculpted. But we wanted it to sound like it exploded out of nowhere."

So where *did* it come from?

Allan Carl Newman—who goes by Carl in his daily life and AC on his solo records—was born on April 14, 1968, in Vancouver, Canada and came of age as indie music tipped toward grunge. Many a young man with a guitar (also, thankfully, a few young women) rushed to join the burgeoning skronkfest, and Newman was no exception.

His first band of note, Superconductor, dropped their debut single, "The Most Popular Man in the World," in '91. It's three minutes and twenty-one seconds of on-trend angst more indebted to Black Francis than Brian Wilson, although hindsight makes clear the dulcet vocal buried within the noise.

Superconductor's debut album, 1993's *Hit Songs for Girls*, continued the aural assault—which, at any given time, featured as many as six guitarists and two bassists—but their second album, 1996's *Bastardsong*, offered a few glimpses of Newman's sonic future. There's still no shortage of overdrive and screaming, but it's punctuated by catchy melodies, multi-tracked vocal harmonies, and unexpected instrumentation. There's even (gasp!) a couple ballads, one of which—the breathtaking, if partially realized, "Cloud Prayer"—would later find its way onto Newman's first solo record.

You'd be forgiven for assuming these shifts represented Newman's early tentative steps toward discovering the sound that would ultimately define his career, but the fact is, he'd already made a quantum leap. See, by the time Superconductor called it quits in '96, Newman's new band, Zumpano, had already released their first album.

Zumpano's *Look What the Rookie Did* came out in 1995 on the venerable indie label Sub Pop. Its follow-up, *Goin' Through Changes*, dropped the next year. Named after their drummer but fronted by Newman, Zumpano was a radical departure for both songwriter and label. Grunge-era skronk was replaced by clever, tuneful sixties guitar pop that presaged, and occasionally bettered, the Shins' 2003 masterpiece, *Chutes Too Narrow*—also notably, a Sub Pop release.

Unfortunately, while the tastemakers at Sub Pop could sense the coming sea change, music fans weren't yet ready to relinquish their distortion. They had no idea what to make of a band that covered Jimmy Webb and sounded like the second coming of the Zombies. And despite their sparkling pop sensibility, Zumpano was often just plain weird. Sure, "Let's Fight" and "The Party Rages On" are bona fide toe-tappers, but tracks like "Snowflakes and Heartaches" and "Some Sun" come off like over-caffeinated Burt Bacharach rave-ups. The latter material might have gained a foothold had it been released in the late aughts alongside Sufjan Stevens' louder offerings, but mid-nineties audiences were baffled. Though now regarded as one of the most underappreciated acts of the decade, Zumpano's records flopped and, soon after, they quietly disbanded.

The New Pornographers began in '97 as a loose collective of likeminded friends: three front people (two of whom, Newman and Bejar, split songwriting duties and played the lion's share of instruments), a drummer, a bassist, and an independent filmmaker who'd taken piano lessons as a child. Legend has it that they took their name from a Jimmy Swaggart quote decrying rock music as the new pornography, but the truth is, Newman was unaware of the quote at the time. (Some versions of the story claim that Swaggart wrote a book titled *Music: The New Pornography*, but—while the quote is real enough, dating back to a televised speech Swaggart gave on June 1, 1986—there is no evidence that any such book exists.) Instead, the name drew inspiration from many sources, including a Japanese film called *The Pornographers* and the sixties folk band the Seekers, who rebranded themselves as the New Seekers when they incorporated rock and roll into their repertoire.

For three years, the New Pornographers recorded in dribs and drabs as their respective schedules allowed. This resulted in heaps of raw material, from which they fashioned *Mass Romantic*.

Listening to *Mass Romantic*—which, to be clear, you should—I can't help but ponder the lessons Newman gleaned from his time with Zumpano. While his lyrics are as wry and enigmatic as they'd ever been, Newman's songs are leaner and more immediate than anything he'd previously recorded. The hooks are hookier. The production is beefier. And the record's oddball moments are largely confined to Bejar's contributions, of which there are four. (Each of the New Pornographers' next five albums would contain three songs written by Bejar; because of scheduling issues, 2017's *Whiteout Conditions* contained none.)

If you're interested in exploring the works of Carl Newman, *Mass Romantic* is an excellent place to start, in part because it's a stellar album without an ounce of chaff, and in part because it serves as a Rosetta Stone of sorts for the remainder of his catalog. Standout songs include the title track and "Letter from an Occupant," both penned by Newman but sung by Neko Case; "The Fake Headlines" and "The Mary Martin Show," on which Newman sings; and Dan Bejar's "Execution Day," although I'd argue Bejar's contributions (to the album, to the band, to the world) are more art rock than power pop and therefore fall outside the purview of this piece.

2003's *Electric Version* is a worthy follow-up to the New Pornographers' acclaimed debut, although—surprisingly, given Newman's artistic restlessness—its pleasures are of a similar sort (see "All for Swinging You Around"). It does, however, iterate in allowing the darkness beneath Newman's bubblegum melodies to occasionally surface, most notably on "From Blown Speakers" and "It's Only Divine Right."

Having established a winning formula, Newman and company spent their next two records subverting it to great effect. *Twin Cinema*, released in 2005, dramatically expanded the New Pornographers' sonic palette, featuring Newman's most anthemic work to date ("Use It," "The Bleeding Heart Show") as well as some of his oddest ("Jessica Numbers," "Stacked Crooked") and sparest ("These Are the Fables"). 2007's *Challengers*—which, for my money, is the band's most underrated album—strikes a pensive, balladic tone that divided critics despite its aching, lovelorn beauty ("Challengers," "My Rights Versus Yours").

Perhaps that's why 2010's *Together* and 2014's *Brill Bruisers* feel a bit like a corrective, a returning to the off-kilter power pop of their first two releases but to slightly diminishing returns. (The latter album's title references New York's Brill Building, where the likes of Neil Diamond, Carole King, and Neil Sedaka penned hits for the teen idols of the sixties.) These albums' relative positions in the New Pornographers canon are largely dependent on the listener's preference for a guitar- (*Together*) or synthesizer-driven (*Brill Bruisers*) sound. Put me down for Team *Together*.

Whiteout Conditions, which came out in 2017, is the first New Pornographers' album penned entirely by Newman. It takes its inspiration from krautrock, cranking up the beats per minute and pushing the synths even further to the fore. That may sound like a radical departure on the page, but in practice, it merely adds a bit of topspin to the New Pornographers' signature style, as the title track makes clear. (Yeah, this piece name checks a lot of Newman's title tracks. What can I say? The guy knows how to pick 'em.)

Newman's first solo album, *The Slow Wonder*, was released in 2004, between *Electric Version* and *Twin Cinema*. He was reportedly so unsure whether his label (Matador, at the time) would have any interest in the album that he applied for a grant from the Canadian government and recorded it in secret. He needn't have worried. Its opening track, "Miracle Drug," is among the catchiest he's ever written and makes a damn fine argument for his inclusion in the power pop firmament all on its own. You could say the same of "Like a Hitman, Like a Dancer" off of 2009's *Get Guilty*. By comparison, "I'm Not Talking" from 2012's

Shut Down the Streets may be a tad down-tempo, but it's a slice of wistful jangle-pop perfection nonetheless. And Newman's solo records contain a wealth of his more esoteric fare, such as *The Slow Wonder*'s "Come Crash" and "The Cloud Prayer" (a version of which first appeared on Superconductor's *Bastardsong*), *Get Guilty*'s "There Are Maybe Ten or Twelve," and *Shut Down the Streets*' "There's Money in New Wave."

Given his bona fides, there's a certain irony in Newman's longtime aversion to being labeled a power pop artist. A talented songwriter with a gift for melody and a fondness for vocal harmonies, he approaches his craft with a magpie sensibility and a knowledge of rock history that rivals any crate-digger's. He counts two patron saints of power pop, Brian Wilson and Paul McCartney (Wings-era, in Newman's case, but still), among his major influences. He speaks openly of his love for Big Star, Cheap Trick, and the Cars. Hell, he's even covered Badfinger in concert. So where, exactly, is the rub?

I think the answer lies in the gulf between the public perception of power pop and the quality of the music the term describes. At root, all genre labels are inherently reductive, but—with the possible exception of emo (a term so frequently and tragically misunderstood, I imagine it spending its days locked in a dark room, listening to itself)—power pop is to music geeks what noir is to crime fiction fans. A source of endless arguments and eye rolls, canonization and revisionism. A phrase so loaded, and so often misused, it pits brother against brother and tears friendships asunder, at least until the booze wears off.

Ask a casual music fan to name a power pop tune, and they're far likelier to say "My Sharona" than "September Gurls." (They're likelier still to erroneously list any number of nineties pop punk radio staples, but that's a topic for another essay.) That's not a knock on the Knack, although I humbly submit that the wildly idiosyncratic nature of their debut single effectively pigeonholed the nascent subgenre—narrowing, rather than expanding, its palette—and the cultural ubiquity of "My Sharona" begat a critical and commercial backlash that tarnished power pop's reputation for decades.

For what it's worth, Newman no longer bristles at being called a power pop artist. "It wasn't until recently that I had someone explain to me what power pop was," he told Cleveland Scene in 2017, by way of explaining his change of heart. "I always thought it was wimpy music made by guys with skinny ties."

Believe me, Carl, I get it. It's easy to be led astray by deceptive packaging. But if you close your eyes and listen, I assure you that you'll know true power pop when you hear it.

Chris Holm *is the author of the cross-genre* Collector *trilogy, the Michael Hendricks thrillers, and thirty-odd short stories in a variety of genres. His work has been selected for The Best American Mystery Stories and named a* New York Times *Editors' Choice; appeared on more than fifty year's best lists; and won a number of awards, including the 2016 Anthony Award for Best Novel.*

Is Weezer Power Pop?

By Daniel Brummel

I DISCOVERED WEEZER AT age twelve thanks to my father, who's always had pretty hip taste in music. He'd already done his due diligence and introduced me to the Beatles; I couldn't get enough of their *1962–1966* compilation (a.k.a. the Red Anthology). Pairing it side-by-side with Weezer's self-titled first record (a.k.a. the Blue Album) felt like that scene in *The Matrix* where Keanu Reeves has to choose between the red and blue pills. I took both—again and again. My mind was blown by the groups' melodic similarities and stylistic differences. I set out to reconcile the musical equation between them, which straddles three decades and an entire genre: power pop.

I was born in 1981, after the first wave of power pop had crested so I don't claim to be an expert. I'm probably only 51 percent conversant in its biggest bands. I have, however, spent a quarter century dissecting the anatomy of Weezer's early albums; indeed, I've existed in a quantum entanglement with "the Weez" for as long as I can remember. Let me divulge some dorky skeletons from deep in my closet…

When "Undone—The Sweater Song" first came into rotation on LA's alt-rock radio station KROQ in '94, I was wrapping up seventh grade, getting interested in young women, rereading

Stephen King's *It* (a meditation on Eddie Cochran's 1958 "Summertime Blues," a power pop ancestor), and diving into my dad's prodigious record collection. An insatiable mediaphile and avid concertgoer since the fifties, Dad dabbled as an organist with his own rock and roll group, the Egg. Having witnessed nearly all the historic rock acts of the twentieth century, he speaks most hyperbolically of the Who. For him, the Who was the greatest live band ever. They were aggressively loud, violently masculine, and explosively incendiary, like the cherry bombs Keith Moon detonated on the Smothers Brothers' show in '67, which deafened Pete Townshend. They were also expansively dynamic and resoundingly harmonic, as in "Pictures of Lily," the onanistic *cosmic egg* that soon hatched into power pop *vérité*.

Dad would often return from record store runs with stacks of used CDs. On one such reconnaissance mission, he procured a promo copy of Weezer's dreamy cerulean blue debut. I compared it to the deeper Beatles cuts I loved, like "I'll Get You" (a pleasantly inexorable threat of fatalistic pursuit) and "I'm Only Sleeping" (which is no soporific jingle). There's real hypnopompic *power* in those tunes; they are simultaneously *perfect power pop* and *emphatically not power pop*, because, like "Pictures of Lily," they are the original, liminal, authentic article. They're the Platonic ideal true power pop worshipped nostalgically when it was birthed in the seventies by acts like Badfinger, first-round Apple Records signees whose name is a Beatles reference and whose final hit "Baby Blue" is quintessential power pop—a position supported by its iconic placement at the final denouement of *Breaking Bad* in 2013.

By the time Henry Winkler (a.k.a. "The Fonz") introduced Weezer at KROQ's Christmas concert in '94, I was utterly hooked on the Blue Album. They blazed through their five-song set at a breakneck clip, and the applause was a deafeningly explosive, unceasing white noise prompting their original bassist Matt Sharp to say, "This is the most insane shit I've ever seen in my life." The only reference point I had for that kind of thunderous adulation was...Beatlemania. It was then I decided I would become a rock musician. Little did I know that twenty years later I'd join Weezer onstage, performing with them at the same Christmas show at the Forum.

◆◆◆

I WAS WEEZER FAN Club member #1642. I've got multiple autographed Weezines, the precious newsletters snail mailed out by presidents Mykel and Carli, who helped us set up local fan club parties, at which my band Ozma performed alongside other startups like Kara's Flowers (now Maroon 5). Mykel and Carli were so sweet and so supportive of us young musicians; the song Rivers named after the duo portrays them impeccably. They even invited me to their home on Burnside Street in Portland, Oregon. When I arrived, they baked me cookies and set me up with a Weezer fangirl I had chatted with on AOL. It was devastating when they were killed in '96, and the memorial show Weezer gave with That Dog was the most heart-wrenching performance I've ever witnessed. It also marked the end of an era for Weezer because it was Matt's last show. Tensions had mounted during the *Pinkerton* sessions (perhaps due to Matt's side project, the Rentals), and Mykel and Carli's deaths were the last straw. Weezer entered a four-year dormancy and was never the same again.

In the interim, Ozma's song "Iceland" opened the *Hear You Me! A Tribute to Mykel and Carli* compilation, and with their posthumous blessing, we inched closer to Weezer. Our guitarist Jose Galvez spotted Rivers at the 2000 Warped Tour and gave him our debut album *Rock and Roll Part Three*. A few weeks later, we heard a report that Rivers was blasting it at home and singing along to every word. This was unbelievable, backwards, and nothing short of miraculous. Then he called to ask if Ozma wanted to open for Weezer in Sacramento. The resounding "Fuck yeah!!!" came from the deepest parts of our beings. Our parents drove up the I-5 together on July 20, 2000, to watch us sound check at the Crest Theatre, presumably to ensure that Weezer wasn't luring us into a hedonistic haven of hookers, blow, timeless melody, and hearing damage.

We then opened for Weezer on two full arena tours, accompanied by the Get Up Kids and Saves the Day, respectively—*emo* bands surfing on the new wave of popularity brought to that subculture by the raw melodrama of Weezer's second record *Pinkerton*. Later, Ozma sailed on both Weezer Cruises and our guitarist Ryen Slegr and I cowrote some tunes with Rivers for Weezer's ninth album, 2014's *Everything Will Be Alright in the End*. NPR dubbed it "Album of the Year," and I joined Weezer as music director and fifth band member for the release tour.

So, my perspective on the question "Is Weezer power pop?" is unique if nothing else, as my entire musical outlook was forged in the furnace of early Beatles and early Weezer as a tweenager. So let's see how the Blue Album's ten tracks shake down on the power pop scale.

"My Name Is Jonas"

A STREAM-OF-CONSCIOUSNESS MEDITATION ON nostalgia kindled by dystopia, set to a heavy waltz. "Wepeel" is Rivers' childhood sled (his Wellesian "Rosebud") while "Jonas" references the protagonist of Lois Lowry's young adult novel *The Giver*, who escapes on his sled from a post-apocalyptic community. The tambourine and arpeggiated acoustic *hemiola* figure hit some stylistic markers of power pop, but the freewheelin' Dylanesque squalling in the harmonica solo belies a more syncretic folk-metal recipe. Dylan was high on the Beats and "thicker'n thieves" with Allen Ginsberg, and the horn-rimmed glasses here are more Ginsberg's than Buddy Holly's—but not necessarily at odds with power pop. John Lennon disclosed in correspondence with Jack Kerouac that the "a" in *The Beatles* was a purposeful Beat Generation reference. The I-V-vi-IV progression (shared with "Let It Be") is milked for all it's worth, then immediately reused in "No One Else." The reliance on amp feedback (like the wild Lydian moment at 0:55) tilts the scales towards Weezer's undeniable metal roots. What a peculiar, enigmatic manifesto to herald a new artist's career! Only 42 percent power pop, though.

"No One Else"

"THE JEALOUS-OBSESSIVE ASSHOLE IN me freaking out on my girlfriend," Rivers declared unabashedly, and indeed these tendencies toward proud possession, misogynistic entitlement, and male privilege are power pop's dirty little secret and its downfall. Consider the 1979 backlash against "My Sharona"— the Knack's pedo-boner—which cannibalized power pop as a commodity. Arenas full of date-rapey jocks chanting this chorus seem dangerously cringeworthy in the wake of the #MeToo movement as men struggle to process the repercussions of predatory behavior (on that note: how was "Run For Your Life" closing out *Rubber Soul* ever condoned?). Again, par for the course in power pop. Musically speaking, the Blue Album's track two is an undeniably relentless barnburner, and Brian Bell's harmony in the final chorus is revelatory. Sixty-nine percent balls-out power pop.

"The World Has Turned And Left Me Here"

THE POSSESSIVE ANTICS HAVE pushed "his girl" away, and the jealous asshole experiences isolation and introversion, existentially contemplating "the void behind my face," perhaps the same void of Lennon's "Tomorrow Never Knows." Wallet photo masturbation is perfectly power pop, an echo of the pornographic "Pictures of Lily." The jangly acoustic arpeggios reappear as rockabilly bluegrass runs ride the galloping beat like a nerdy cowboy on a heavy metal horse, while the backup harmonies channel Brian Wilson (Rivers is a self-professed Beach Boys freak who proclaimed that "I Just Wasn't Made For These Times" is the "most ultimately beautiful pop music"). A bit "heady," so to speak, but still 62 percent power pop.

"Buddy Holly"

...IS HIMSELF A RECOGNIZED power pop precursor. The Beatles' very first recording (as the Quarrymen) was his "That'll Be the Day" in 1958. And I'd pay to hear Weezer cover "Everyday," whose long flowing melodies, boyish hiccups, and sugary glockenspiel solo are more *pure pop* than *power pop*. By channeling him, Rivers tapped deeply into a powerful bespectacled American musical archetype—a smart choice, as his original lyric name-checking Ginger Rogers and Fred Astaire wouldn't have hit as hard. Male insecurity, twisted violence, and patronizing condescension creep through the verses, vanquished by the celebrity lookalike chorus. The quirky Korg keyboard lines show Ric Ocasek's *new wave* imprint and power pop pedigree—thank God he convinced the band this song wasn't too cheesy to include on the album! *Rolling Stone's* Laura Braun pointed to this song specifically when she wrote that the Blue Album "charmed listeners across genres with catchy radio-ready power pop tunes." The nine-note lick that catapults us out of the guitar solo into the stratosphere seals the deal: 92 percent power pop.

"Undone—The Sweater Song"

THE FIRST WEEZER SONG ever written and a conscious attempt to mimic the Velvet Underground—art rock or proto-punk for sure, but definitely not power pop! VU gave "The Gift" of spoken word; the voices working out rides to the after party are Matt Sharp, roadie extraordinaire Karl Koch, and fan club sweetheart Mykel Allan. Then, more existential Beat poetry (this time exploring Cartesian dualism, like any geek rocker should) over an off-kilter, major-six-sharp-nine riff acknowledged as "almost a complete rip-off" of Metallica's "Welcome Home (Sanitarium)." The dada prepared piano outro is less "Revolution" and more "Revolution 9." All this trippy oddness is more Pavement than Plimsouls, driving down the power pop quotient…only jangly in a slanted-enchanted sort of way. Modulating up a minor third for the solo is straight out of the Kinks' playbook though, and the chorus changes are identical to the Kingsmen's "Louie Louie," a milestone on the road between garage rock and power pop. Rivers said "it perfectly encapsulates Weezer to me—you're trying to be cool like Velvet Underground, but your metal roots just pump through unconsciously." Barely 49 percent power pop, and if this is Rivers' definitive Weezer song, the band as a whole might fall just short of membership in the genre.

"Surf Wax America"

THE OPENING RIFF SOUNDS more rockabilly than surf, like it fell out of Dwight Twilley's guitar case on his way to record "I'm On Fire" (whose bridge echoes "Norwegian Wood"). There's a Californian cowboy here. His smug choice of surfboard as basic transportation might well be substituted for horse and saddle. The requisite violent aggression box is checked—it's snotty and pissy, ramps into a Maidenesque gallop, and culminates in imminent death in the riptide. Drummer Pat Wilson's punk blast beats up the ante on tempo from the sauntering, swaggering grooves of traditional power pop. The Beach Boys influence is paramount here, thematically as well as harmonically in the stony vocal breakdown. Smoke dope! Eighty-four percent power pop and proud.

"Say It Ain't So"

THAT CHARMINGLY DISSONANT MAJOR-SHARP-NINE chord from "Undone" appears again; its bent vibe pairs well with the theme of generational alcohol use and abuse. There's a touch of Jimi Hendrix in the bluesy faux-jazz licks, and incisive syncopated reggae chanks set up the hugely heavy chorus crashes, flanked by feedback. The bridge resolving by tritone into the guitar solo is one of the most jarring shifts accepted in recent popular music (although a similar move gets used in the chorus to "Only In Dreams"). Not so much power pop—19 percent.

"In The Garage"

SEE "IN MY ROOM," if you're a Beach Boy. The introverted headspace is power pop enough, but then Rivers expressly names his favorite band KISS, confirming Weezer's heavy metal core. KISS's "shock rock" antics are paralleled in Weezer's ambivalent embrace of gimmickry, and the way that the Blue Album toes the "joke band" line (whereas power pop is a more earnest style). We're harmonica-heavy again here—and though it's used incidentally in the Romantics' "What I Like About You," the Knack's "Good Girls Don't," and Big Star's "Life Is White," to my ears, early Weezer relies on harmonica in a way that harkens back to a time before power pop. And the Dungeons & Dragons references scream "Geek rock! Nerd rock! Dork rock!" A related, but more precocious and specific style. Fifty-eight percent power pop.

"Holiday"

SEE "ON A HOLIDAY," if you're a Beach Boy. The first line "Let's go away for a while" references the gorgeous *Pet Sounds* instrumental of the same name. Beat poetry reappears as Rivers calls out Kerouac by name; and it doesn't get much geekier than the "bivouac" slant rhyme. The stacked "heartbeat" harmonies and cocksure delivery make this actually pretty darn power pop—88 percent.

"Only In Dreams"

LENGTH ALONE PULLS THIS one out of power pop contention— tight song structures are a power pop prerequisite that Weezer frequently eschews. Traces of jazz can be heard in the improvisatory, impressionistic approach, and around 6:10 it gets impressively dissonant as the guitars bend into microtones recalling the über-futuristic approach of space rockers Hum (who are probably only three or four percent power pop themselves). Only 12 percent power pop.

◆◆◆

THERE ARE A FEW scattered power pop moments in Weezer's post-Blue catalog—think "(If You're Wondering If I Want You To) I Want You To" off of *Raditude,* or the sublime *Pinkerton* B-sides "I Just Threw Out the Love of my Dreams" and "Devotion"— but they generally didn't get any *more* power pop as their career pressed on. Averaging the above scores gives us a power pop quotient of 57.5 percent for the Blue Album as a whole. So while Weezer probably doesn't quite qualify as a power pop band on the whole, they may have started out as one with the Blue Album.

Daniel Brummel, M.M. *is perhaps best known as the leader of the power pop-influenced groups Ozma and Sanglorians, and has also performed in Weezer, Nada Surf, Spain, and the Elected. He is a veteran music educator who holds bachelor's and master's degrees in music composition, and he composes the music for Jenji Kohan's new Renaissance Faire dramedy,* American Princess. *Formerly the dean at the California College of Music, Daniel now serves as the Chief Academic Officer of Point Blank Music School in Silver Lake, California.*

Excerpts from Scott Miller's Music: What Happened?

By Scott Miller, with an introduction by Paul Myers

*L*ONG BEFORE *I* MOVED *to San Francisco in 1997, I had been aware of the quirky genius of Scott Miller, ever since a record store clerk friend back in Toronto had slipped into my bag a "free" copy of an album called* Lolita Nation *by Miller's band, Game Theory. My power pop radar perked up immediately upon hearing the song "Nothing New," which seemed to marry slacker indie rock cool with post-Robyn Hitchcock/Syd Barrett obtuse wit, and yet sounded wholly and uniquely American. Once I'd settled in to life in the Bay Area, I became pals with some of the people in his scene, particularly Game Theory's charming and tasteful drummer Gil Ray, now sadly departed, and Alison Faith Levy, who played keyboards in Miller's next band, the Loud Family. It still took me a few years to actually meet Scott himself, but my moment came in 2010 after the publication of my book about Todd Rundgren's studio productions,* A Wizard, A True Star, *which coincided with Miller's own book of capsule record reviews,* Music: What Happened? *With Alison's help, Scott and I agreed to do a joint book release concert, Wizards And Stars, featuring a gang of Bay Area artists covering Rundgren songs, with a special solo set featuring Scott performing electric versions of selected songs from his book. It went so well that* we recreated the concept down in LA the following March at Largo at the Coronet, cohosted by me and comedian Dave Foley (Kids In The Hall) and a cast that included Jon Brion, Mike Viola, Lyle Workman, The Section String Quartet, and by Scott's invitation, Aimee Mann. My duo with John Moremen, the Paul & John, got to back Scott on a majestically sloppy cover of Rundgren's "Couldn't I Just Tell You," and Scott wrote something nice in the inside flap of my copy of Music: What Happened? I would end up interacting with Scott infrequently over the next two years, until news broke of his sudden and tragic death by suicide on April 15, 2013, at the age of fifty-three, which continues to leave a hole in the lives of his wife and two young daughters, his many close friends and musical colleagues, countless fans, and those who knew him only a little.

In tribute to Scott, who counted great power pop among the many musical forms he admired and employed, we have included a few relevant entries from Music: What Happened? in no particular order.

"No Matter What" Badfinger

THIS IS MORE PROPERLY power pop and arguably the first of a handful of the true power pop masterpieces. Soundwise, it's a joyous, overdriven throbbing of all things analog. What sets this apart from many pretenders to the throne is Pete Ham's rich, resonant voice; he doesn't sound like a kid. Likewise, this isn't confession of adolescent feelings, this is laying down a commitment. One of many things that weren't understood well enough in Badfinger's time was their sense of gravity.

"Day After Day" Badfinger

IN THEIR TIME, BADFINGER suffered under the judgment that they perpetuated an earlier Beatles style from which the world had moved on, rendering the likes of the bona fide George Harrison participation here double-edged swords. Soon enough, two of the members killed themselves. And now, hey, they're actually the band from this era who sound fresh, like Big Star. There's a strange tragic weight to all of that. *Straight Up* is their strongest album, and "Day After Day" was their song that was the biggest part of my life at the time.

"Couldn't I Just Tell You" Todd Rundgren

SOMETHING/ANYTHING WAS A MILESTONE in record albums' ability to achieve direct and intimate personal communication. It accomplished it with frankly light fare (like "I Saw the Light" and "Hello, It's Me") and frankly humorous diversions (like "Wolfman Jack"), but the way it modulates over its two albums to weightier material—"the kid gets heavy," as I believe the album puts it—is nuanced and moving in and of itself. "Couldn't I Just Tell You" arrives as Todd has loaded the bases in a way that will never quite be the same again and hits one out of the park. Likely the greatest power pop recording ever made, it's somehow both desperate and lighthearted at the same time—with both the believable abandonment of "you can turn your back whenever you please" and the confessional cleverness of "I'm not a coward if that's what you believe" and "couldn't we pretend that it's no big deal?" The guitar solo features some truly amazing dexterity and inflection, and that open-string reinvention of the theme near the end is simply awesome. He'd probably thank you to remember that he's a guitar great, and the evidence is right here.

"Earn Enough for Us" XTC

XTC WERE NOTORIOUSLY FURIOUS with Todd Rundgren's excellent production. I've never known the details and always been curious. I mean, the mind reels at the potential for bad ideas Todd could be capable of embracing unreservedly, but this doesn't sound like any of those. Let's see there's no hideous but oddly cool graphic-EQ snare sound, no soul numbers, nothing obviously done on a laptop; could there have been motorcycles and lace sleeves involved? While I like this song's charming and catchy take on wedded bliss in hard economic times, I don't share the general enthusiasm for, say, the hit "Dear God" (nothing against the sentiment, which happens to be lame, but the tune just doesn't do it for me); I'd rather send newcomers to the masterful *Drums and Wires*, *English Settlement*, or *Oranges and Lemons* as whole albums.

"2020" The Orange Peels

One of the most delectable power pop melodies in years comes from a group I've—obviously—never paid the right amount of attention to before. It doesn't hurt that they've spent their time doing the work it takes to sound like a million bucks: crack production, dynamite lead vocals with a kicker payload of wicked vibrato; the whole album is gloriously well-crafted. There's a mysterious golden-mean quality to the way "2020"'s 6/8 verse works so well. It's almost an A-B-A-A pattern, which is to say, almost anticlimactic on paper that turns out to be a fist-pumper in real life.

"Back of a Car" Big Star

There's a good chance *Radio City* is the best album not by the Beatles; it's hard to evaluate the way one does other contenders like *Who's Next* or *This Year's Model* because those albums made a big splash, and *Radio City* went so completely neglected on initial release (I didn't know about Big Star until 1980). It's hard to describe how certain I was, almost immediately, of the record's greatness. Auteur Alex Chilton typically disavows that much specialness; he once said something like, "Those are just the chords your hands want to play on guitar if you've been at it a certain length of time." That (probably botched) quote is just more specialness to me: sorry, Alex, vicious cycle. The second, diminished chord of "Back of a Car" is palpably unlikely except maybe in 1920s blues, although, you know what?—your hands do like to play it. Maybe it's about doing what your hands want. Besides the music, the sound engineering of *Radio City*, its sheer management of tremendous energy in the high end is incredible. Here's one where I insist on the vinyl source, which achieves a combination of depth and luster that, if you just look at the graphic EQ, would spell thin and hissy in almost any other recording. Yet, there's a cradling, bass guitar–dominated low end that somehow reads to the ear as big without being high volume. The lyrics of Radio City are an interesting analog to the mind-grabbing Bill Eggleston photo of the red-ceilinged room on the cover. That black light astro-sign sex position poster occupies the same realm of gently scrutinized artifacts of youth as the whirring teen thoughts in the lyrics: "Sitting in the back of a car / Music so loud I can't tell a thing / Thinking about what to say / And I can't find the lines." Alex was of course at least as dismissive of the lyrics as the music, and it's possible to see that he wasn't going for articulation of marginalized teen vulnerability, nor probably taking any of the kind of literary aim that could hit a target by Like Flies on Sherbert: no youth-speak pastiche on *Radio City* is as witty as "My rival, he drives a Triumph sports car, has muscles, and is a deceitful person." One impressive twist is "I know I'll feel a whole lot more when I get alone." There's a rare astuteness about that. Then there's the patented Chilton wrong yet strangely right diction of "I'll go on and on with you / Like to fall and lie with you." Why is that so good? There's a longing in there for a sexual connection to act as a leap of faith a context, in which words fail by nature, except that here in Alex's little song, maybe they don't quite fail.

"Andy, Please" Van Duren

RECORDED IN 1978 AND unreleased until 2003, *Idiot Optimism* is part two of Van Duren's brief but bright two-year recording career. "Andy, Please" exists in demo form, I believe with minor deity Jody Stephens in semi-permanent drummer capacity just after Big Star. Vocally callow and in some ways with more power pop sense (the line "I'm aware of the love you're going through" has something Chilton-worthy about it), the demo is worth seeking out; this album version has some boring studio pro guitar and a gravellier vocal that in the end is just so good you have to call it the definitive version.

"Black and White" The dB's

CHRIS STAMEY'S B-SIDE "SOUL KISS" grabbed me first: "Yes, your party dress/It was my obsession/Now I'm impervious to that / It's your soul kiss, that's what I miss." I think that was my very first marveling at the devilry with words and music that was Chris's gift. But "Black and White" is in its own way just as nervy, and arguably the first college rock classic. The string arpeggio style has to have been formative for Pete Buck. Drummer Will Rigby and bassist Gene Holder do amazing work here, too.

"Teenage FBI" Guided By Voices

RIC OCASEK WAS AN epiphany as the choice to produce the first Weezer album, and for what my two cents are worth, it's almost as symbiotic a match here. After the several high points of *Mag Earwhig!*, a breakthrough Guided By Voices song seemed within striking distance, and to me, "Teenage FBI" is every inch that classic. It took me some introspection to realize this, given the widespread hostility to *Do the Collapse*. I guess it's just very easy for the story to be that GBV were put on earth to make "low-fi" home level recordings until killjoy Ric Ocasek came along with a big bag of not getting it. Or Bob had just stirred up the right amount of bad blood. But disliking "Teenage FBI" is just wrong. The musicians I know who have an opinion love it enough to cover it with enthusiasm. No points for Pitchfork here.

"My Blank Pages" Velvet Crush

By 1993, A LOT of bands had figured out that it was okay to be a guitar band again, and in 1994, some were deciding it was okay to be a heavy guitar band again. You still couldn't be outright hair metal, no doubt to much secret chagrin, but ironic postmodern nostalgia made for a leash long enough to sneak in some Hendrix, as with Soundgarden or Lenny Kravitz. This, when you did the math, was another way of stating the curious fact that new bands could only be alternative bands; there was no longer any such thing as being whatever this was the alternative to. Classic rock radio was of course really big, and non-ironic, but whereas in 1984, the average teenage loud guitar band was actually prepared for Foreigner covers to figure into their early career path, ten years later anything like that was gone from the world. Situated on the album *Teenage Symphonies to God*, "My Blank Pages" reminds us there was a hard guitar rock strain that cared about the Byrds and Brian Wilson (famous "symphonies" quote), and not much about grunge.

"Seems So" Apples in Stereo

Pure pop doesn't get any more blindingly enjoyable than this. There's almost something of a Jerome Kern confection in the whole-step descents, as well as more obvious channeling of 1965 Beatles and Byrds. The cycles through the "dozed off on my pillow," "whole thing from my window" pattern hit with such miraculous perfection that you're put under the temporary impression that no one else is doing music quite right.

"The Man I Used to Be" Jellyfish

Per their version of postmodernism, Jellyfish telegraphed a compelling appreciation of production values ripe for revisiting, from their H.R. Pufnstuf wardrobe to their bright selection of Saturday Night Fever producer Albhy Galuten for their debut album. Especially with Jason Falkner in the lineup, they were the right people to produce a quality result, too; my band rehearsed across the hallway from them for a long time, and you could hear them literally practicing the same three-second vocal cluster for an hour.

"Carrie Anne" The Hollies

This one is in some ways the benchmark power pop song. It's very simple, for one thing.

Anything by the Raspberries is a concerto by comparison; for the first British Invasion bands, the soil hadn't been farmed to death yet. I mean, the chorus hits, there's a big vocal fourth, right on the downbeat, with the word "hey"! All power pop wants to do this. Then, but for the Hollies having done it first, it wants to say a girl's name. Then, ask her what her game is. And then it could hardly be expected to stop itself from wanting to play.

"Map Ref. 41'N 93'W" Wire

THERE WERE ONLY VAGUE hints that Wire were one day going to be capable of music this ravishing. "Outdoor Miner" maybe? Better yet, it's a great sound built from unlikely materials: squelching, modulated synths, disembodied riffs, Colin Newman's uningratiating reading. I don't recognize any particular narrative, just an ominous evocation of loss associated with the way some land is being subjected to mapping of its borders. The mood struck initially is not much more than irksome, a mood to play on the word "rule"—"an unseen ruler defines...an unrulable expanse of geography"—but the effects become more grave: "beneath the rule a country hides." By the end, "a deep breath of submission has begun." Off the top of my head, the best piece of art rock.

Paul Myers *is a Toronto, Canada born, and Berkeley, California based writer and musician who has written for* Mojo, MIX, Crawdaddy, *and* Fast Company, *and is the author of four books, including* A Wizard A True Star: Todd Rundgren In The Studio *and most recently* Kids In The Hall: One Dumb Guy, *in 2018. His short autobiographical piece, the Cherokee Record Club, appeared in Rare Bird's 2013 prog rock anthology,* Yes Is The Answer.

Scott Miller *(April 4, 1960–April 15, 2013) was a singer, songwriter and guitarist, best known for his work as leader of the 1980s band* Game Theory *and 1990s band* The Loud Family. *In 2010, 125 Books published a collection of his music criticism,* Music: What Happened? *In 2014, Omnivore Recordings began reissuing the entire* Game Theory *catalog, including the posthumously completed* Supercalifragile, *in 2017.*

Surrender

By Marko DeSantis

POWER POP MIGHT BE the most inconvenient genre in rock and roll. Early on, my band Sugarcult was alternately *accused of* and *celebrated for* being kinda power pop. Still, it's safe to say that nobody ever got laid (or paid) by claiming to be power pop, unless they were called the Knack.

Rock and roll has endured its fair share of schisms, reformations, and splits ever since it broke outta the bad part of town, crossed the railroad tracks, liberated teenage pelvises, popped the cherry of midcentury American innocence, and subsequently saved our souls. Most people know what you mean by: hard rock, heavy metal, punk, grunge, indie, pop, and even pop punk. But power pop...*what'd you call me?!*

I might be wrong to even call it a genre. Power pop could instead be seen as a recurring correction (or affliction!) that happens to rock and roll every so often. When rock music shows symptoms of straying too far off course from its baseline *3-chords and something to say* trajectory, sooner or later along comes Big Star, Flamin' Groovies, Ramones, Cheap Trick, Buzzcocks, the Cars, Elvis Costello, the Knack, Plimsouls, Tom Petty, the Replacements, Redd Kross, the Best Kissers in the World, Cheap Trick again, Teenage Fanclub, the Muffs, Weezer, sorta Nirvana and Green Day, Superdrag, Fountains of Wayne, Tsar, OK Go, Best Coast, and (reliably) Cheap Trick *again*, to save the day!

Most contemporary bands that get called power pop immediately dodge the classification in order to avoid the likelihood of forsaking their chances of having a go at mainstream success. Instead, they wisely assimilate neatly into more user-friendly categories like indie rock, modern rock, pop rock, and such. The few groups that attempt to wear power pop as a badge of underground cool on the lapels of their secondhand suit jackets seem doomed to cult status at best, show up on some blogs year end/best-of lists and eventually tire of the fleeting romantic allure of endless van tours, tongue-in-cheek Thanksgivings at Waffle House, well drinks, and cheap motels.

Maybe there's the occasional scene of cool kids that get it, but usually these bands are relegated to the curiosities of insufferable divorced dudes who spend their midlife crises hanging out at resurgent vinyl shops extolling the virtues of Jellyfish and defending other-than-*Frosting on the Beater* Posies records to some aspiring bassist working behind the counter, wearing an Earthless T-shirt and politely doing the best he can not to completely nod off.

But that's part of the all-inclusive fun of being a music fan anyway; you can go in through the front door and get with what's on mainstream terrestrial radio and/or go around back and dumpster dive into the brilliant obscurities and esoteric also-rans. The latter might initially be a decidedly more lonesome (and celibate) pursuit, but it can be some wild fun nonetheless.

So, what in the actual fuck is power pop anyway? Well, what ISN'T power pop? I mean, most of the bands people call power pop exhibit most of the usual characteristics emblematic of rock music—simple melodies, hooks, riffs, harmonies, pop arrangements, loud guitars/bass/drums, etc. I think it's a simple case of: *If you know, you know.*

Y'know, right?

So, for now, since it's almost last call, let's put on some records (I love that recent band Beach Slang; that new Green Day spinoff called the Longshot; or that ill-fated nineties group the Exploding Hearts) and just co-opt what Louis Armstrong said about jazz, for our beloved, misunderstood flag-without-a-nation of a genre: "If you have to ask... You'll never know!"

Call it power pop, or call it late for supper. In the end, it's about the music, the artists, the songs, the feelings evoked, and the context in which we experience the whole shebang. I've come full circle with Sugarcult and accepted that rock and roll is too vague, and by swerving to avoid being pegged as one thing, you become vulnerable to worse evils from critics who will gladly place you in the box of their choosing. In our case, we got stuck with such lame default settings as pop punk, emo, and pop rock. We may have sold a few extra hoodies to suburban teens in flyover states as a result, but we got dismissed by a lot of discerning music fans with preconceived notions. So, I surrender: Sugarcult is a power pop band, and for better or for worse, we've probably been one all along.

Marko DeSantis *is a music professional best known as the lead guitarist and cofounder of Sugarcult. The band released three records, spawning radio singles such as "Bouncing Off the Walls" and "Memory." He has toured worldwide and sold over a million records since launching out of Santa Barbara, California. Marko has also played in power pop/punk bands such as Popsicko, the Ataris, Swingin Utters, Bad Astronaut, the Playing Favorites, and Nerf Herder. Currently, Marko is a professor at several top music colleges (MI, LACM, and Citrus) where he lectures on music business and songwriting. Marko DeSantis is based in Los Angeles, California.*

From Pop Punk to Power Pop

By Kurt Baker

M Y FIRST BAND, THE Leftovers, began as your stereotypical high school punk outfit, chugging twenty-four packs of Vanilla Coca-Cola in our twice-per-week rehearsals after school in the basement of my parents' house. If you told us that seven years later we'd be playing on stage to a sold-out crowd at the Roundhouse in London, we would've laughed and been like, "Yeah, why not?" We were determined and wanted to succeed, but by our own rules and with our own sound.

That meant following the scriptures of the Ramones, Green Day, Screeching Weasel, and the Queers. Timing was right because the pop punk scene was experiencing a bit of a renaissance in the mid aughts, but we ended up taking the pop side of "pop punk" a bit too far—which would ultimately be our demise. Being the main songwriter of the group, I bear the responsibility for that stylistic shift. Friendships were shattered and feelings were hurt as I got a fresh start with power pop thanks to influences like Elvis Costello, the Romantics, the Rubinoos, and more.

As a passionate music fan connecting those dots, noticing the musical similarities, and finding my place in it all was a predestined journey for me. I'm still on that journey today, currently fronting the Kurt Baker Combo from my home base in Madrid. And I've got no regrets about it.

♦♦♦

THE ONE ALBUM THAT opened my eyes to the connection between pop punk and power pop was *21st Century Power Pop Riot*, released by Chicago punk band the Methadones in 2006. An entire album of cover songs from the glory days of power pop done in the Methadones' punk fashion was a revelation for me. The band covers each song with ease and grace, keeping the feeling of the original, but giving it their personal touch—stripped down production, loud guitars, and increased tempo.

The end result is a covers collection that feels like an album of original songs, a feat not easy to pull off. This probably has a lot to do with the DNA of the original arrangements. Songs like "Out of Luck" by Pointed Sticks and Joe Jackson's "I'm The Man" were, in essence, the pop punk songs of the late seventies with their simple chord structures, wonderful melodies, and full-on attitude.

The Methadones formed in Chicago in the nineties, but didn't kick into full gear until lead singer and songwriter Dan Schafer (a.k.a. Danny Vapid) left the seminal pop punk band Screeching Weasel. Schafer came and went as a bassist/guitarist for Screeching Weasel from that time, but always perfectly complimented the snotty vocals of front man Ben Foster (a.k.a. Ben Weasel).

For the uninitiated, Screeching Weasel is one of the iconic pop punk groups from the nineties. Along with the Queers and the Mr. T Experience, they paved the way for bands like Blink 182, MxPx, and Green Day. The common thread with these Lookout Records bands was their love for the Ramones who, in my opinion, set the blueprint for putting the "pop" into "punk."

The Ramones, along with contemporaries like the Buzzcocks and the Dickies, were huge influences on Schafer and Foster, who used the same template for the poppier Screeching Weasel songs. But Screeching Weasel wasn't only influenced by punk bands. It might have been their upbringing in seventies suburban Chicago that exposed them to great local power pop acts as well. Bands like Cheap Trick, Off Broadway, Pezband, and Shoes make themselves known in hooky Screeching Weasel songs like "Guest List" or "Around On You."

◆◆◆

THINGS DIDN'T PICK UP for the Leftovers until Ben Weasel wrote a rave review of our single "Steppin' On My Heart" on his blog. (We couldn't believe he was a fan.) With his approval, we began getting European tour offers and started opening up for the Queers on coast-to-coast US jaunts. I owe a lot to Ben for this, but it wasn't until I got to know the guys from Screeching Weasel that I realized I had more in common musically with Weasel's bandmate, Dan.

During the recording session for the Leftovers album *On the Move*, I bought a copy of *On!* by Off Broadway. Dan and I became friends through our mutual love of Off Broadway and decided to write a couple songs together. It's a lasting pop punk friendship formed over the love of a Chicago power pop band.

Off Broadway's debut album is in the same vein as Cheap Trick's *In Color* or *Heaven Tonight*, largely due to the production work of Tom Werman. Both bands came from the same scene, but Off Broadway never found the same level of commercial success. Interestingly, it was Cheap Trick that led me to Off Broadway.

I got into Cheap Trick after high school, around the same time as the *On the Move* sessions. They had the same urgency, danger, and velocity of my favorite punk bands but were more influenced by the Beatles and sixties psych. One of my favorite Cheap Trick songs is "He's a Whore" from their self-titled debut (later covered on the Methadones' *21st Century Power Pop Riot*). The Methadones' version really brings out the underlying punk attitude and grit, making it clear how suburban Chicago kids could go from listening to Cheap Trick in 1977 to the Ramones *Leave Home* in 1978 without a jump of the needle.

I already owned records by Cheap Trick, Joe Jackson, the Pointed Sticks, Nick Lowe, and Elvis Costello when the Methadones released *21st Century Power Pop Riot* in 2006. But that album pushed me over the edge. For legal reasons, the Methadones' album didn't include lyrics and songwriters in the liner notes, which led me on a quest to collect LPs by the original artists.

◆◆◆

WHEN IT COMES TO my own personal power pop odyssey, if it weren't for the Beatles and the World Wide Web, I might have ended up listening to rap/rock or reggeaton. In 2019, I've got different opinions about the internet, but I still love the Beatles just as much as the first time I heard them when I was five years old. I remember the exact moment my uncle popped in a cassette tape—the opening piano line from "The Word" and everything that followed completely consumed me. The Beatles' lyrics and melodies shaped my musical tastes from that point forward. Beatles fans are often religious in their devotion to the band and their music. If that's the case, then power pop bands are the true disciples. I am proud to be one of them.

So, with the Beatles as my starting point, I gravitated to oldies radio, which in the nineties was mostly fifties and sixties pop. Punk rock biographies taught me that early seventies music was pure sludge, but I had to disagree. Luckily, the Ramones bridged the gap between pop punk and sixties rock for me because they idolized groups like the Beach Boys, the Turtles, and the Dave Clark Five. Those pop influences spoke to me too and started to show up in some of my own songwriting toward the end of the Leftovers.

Tensions were high during the recording of our last album, *Eager to Please,* with producer Linus Dotson (a.k.a. Linus of Hollywood) in 2008. Our drummer would storm out of the sessions because he felt things were getting too "pop"—which was true. The songs had been highly influenced by the Rubinoos, who I heard for the first time while on tour in Italy. The Rubinoos' tight vocal melodies and infectious hooks drew me in like a tractor beam. As soon as I got home from Europe, I went out and bought every Rubinoos album I could find.

We even had their lead vocalist, Jon Rubin, sing on our cover of the Rubinoos' song "Party Till We Die." I was thrilled, but the other guys in the Leftovers weren't having it. They wanted to stay a pop punk band, with the emphasis on *punk.* The Leftovers were done a year later. It's a cliché to cite "musical differences" as the reason for a band breakup, but in our case it was true. As a songwriter, I was getting tired of the straightforward, three-chord approach. I was feeling boxed in and searching for something more; something that combined catchy melodies with a punk rock attitude. I found that with power pop.

I immersed myself in music blogs and discovered some glorious songs from the late seventies and early eighties by the Shivvers, the Secrets, Nikki and the Corvettes, Paul Collins, Phil Seymour, Artful Dodger, and many more. There were so many hidden gems out there that never got the respect they deserved. So when Oglio Records approached me about doing a power pop covers album, it was a no brainer. The result is *Got It Covered.*

◆◆◆

Touchdown LAX. I was thrilled to begin recording my first solo release in Los Angeles, a town that's so different from where I grew up in Maine. The palm trees and the sun—the vibe, the feeling, and the people—even the rough edges have a certain charm to them. It was the perfect place to record *Got It Covered* because of all the legendary music recorded there. Brian Wilson, the Wrecking Crew, Jan and Dean…the Knack! I checked into my hotel right behind the Chinese Theater and immediately began my transformation.

It was an important trip for me. I was becoming something other than a pop punk musician. Maybe it goes back to my days in children's theater, but I wanted to dress the part too—to get into character for this next musical phase. I put myself in the shoes of Doug Fieger or Elvis Costello, wearing a suit jacket and skinny tie to all the recording sessions.

I narrowed down a list of cover songs for the album, kicking off with "Let Me Out" by the Knack. I originally hoped to record a few more obscure power pop covers, but we ended up with a list of songs that were pretty well known. This was challenging because the original versions were hard to beat. I had to remind myself that the objective of a good cover is not to improve on the song, but to interpret it in a new way. The original "Let Me Out" is a perfect song from a perfect album. The Knack version is played with tight precision and force, so I wanted my cover of it to up the ante. I'll let you decide if I pulled it off!

With Linus of Hollywood producing and playing guitar and Adam Marcello on drums, we had everything we needed to make an exciting album. I'm proud of it because you can hear how much fun we had when you listen to our version of songs like "Pump It Up." Linus created a stress-free atmosphere in the studio that never felt rushed—very different from my previous studio experiences with the Leftovers. Linus and I have similar musical tastes, so a lot of time was just spent drinking beer and talking about how much we loved the songs we were recording.

I was so at ease that *Got It Covered* still contains some of my favorite vocal performances. "Is She Really Going Out With Him?" and "I've Done Everything for You" were two songs that I had always wanted to sing. It was easy to get into the mindset of Joe Jackson or Rick Springfield, trying to mix their original vocal delivery with my own personality. Those songs are covers, but they represent some powerful influences for me.

"Hanging on the Telephone" was originally written by Jack Lee and performed by the Nerves, but I grew up with the Blondie version. To this day, whenever the Kurt Baker Combo plays this tune while backing up Paul Collins of the Nerves around Europe, I still find myself inadvertently strumming the Blondie version by mistake. But for me, the cover I'm most proud of is "Cruel to be Kind." Nick Lowe has always been a favorite, and I really wanted to do a version that showed how much I loved the song.

When I arrived back in Maine after the recording session, I got together with my friends at our favorite local watering hole, Ruski's. After a couple rounds and some catching up, I took out this portable camcorder and we shot a music video that showcases my town and my friends. These folks are people I love and admire, and they were the ones that were there for me when I was feeling blue about the Leftovers breaking up. With *Got It Covered*, I had a great starting point for my new musical journey.

Since *Got It Covered*, I've released several solo records. I made a few with musicians and friends in the States and others with my group, the Kurt Baker Combo, in Spain. I didn't think I'd find myself recording "power pop" music when I first heard the Beatles, but here I am today. I've been grateful for all the support and the kind words, but I have to admit that—just like with pop punk—I sometimes feel boxed in by the power pop label.

These days I simply describe my music as rock and roll. The reality is that despite all the labels put on my albums, I've always loved good melodies and catchy hooks. Rock and roll for me is all about freedom, about doing what you want and following your passions. My passion is music—creating songs that people remember and can dance too. Call it power pop, or rock and roll, or whatever. I'm just happy that I found out who I am and what I love to do. I'll be forever grateful for the opportunity to keep on pursuing that passion.

Kurt Baker *is a musician, producer, multi-instrumentalist and music fan from Portland, Maine. He is best known for his work with* The Leftovers, *his solo album* Brand New Beat *and power pop covers album* Got It Covered. *Currently, he resides in Madrid, Spain, where he fronts The Kurt Baker Combo who have released two full-length records on Little Steven Van Zandt's Wicked Cool Records. When not on tour or in the studio, Baker enjoys cooking and watching old episodes of* Murder She Wrote.

Liz Phair the Poptimist

By Carrie Courogen

THE EARLY AUGHTS WEREN'T exactly a media landscape that endeared itself to my parents. It was the heyday of Total Request Live, when Britney became a "bad girl" and Christina joined her, when Hilary Duff turned her TV starpower into a music career, and Jessica Simpson turned her music career into a TV show. Our TV was enforced by parental controls, and once Britney held that snake, my music television access was limited to VH1, whose programming was heavy on aging seventies rock stars' safe, adult contemporary output and not much else. MTV had to be consumed in bits and pieces, after school at friends' houses or sleepovers. It was during one of those covert viewings that I heard Liz Phair's "Extraordinary" for the first time. It felt like a revelation.

Phair's confidence was infectious; her defiant proclamation of being flawed but still spectacular was a riveting message I'd yet to receive from a song. The pop music my friends and I consumed as twelve-year-olds lacked this sort of feeling. The closest thing girls our age had to an empowerment anthem at the time was Kelly Clarkson's "Miss Independent." But Clarkson, whose music was fizzy and fun, was a reality show winner. Her career was launched in part by a panel of three judges (two of them men) and call-in votes. How powerful was that?

But Phair seemed different. She seemed like a big sister I didn't have. She was cool, but not too cool; confident, but not so much that she seemed unapproachable. There was something both comforting and empowering about the way she sang about herself, about the shit she took and gave right back. Maybe those bro-y guys you grow up with would never change as you became adults, but maybe you can learn to stand up for yourself. I would later branch further into her deep discography, but 2003's *Liz Phair* was my— and many other millennial women's—much-needed introduction.

By the time *Liz Phair* was released, power pop was largely a thing of the past. Despite a brief resurgence in the mid-nineties, by 2003, power pop was a moniker most often associated with bands from the late seventies and early eighties. Mainstream radio overlooked nuance in favor of anyone who fit neatly into three clearly defined strains of rap, pop, or rock. The indie hipster market, who had once championed Phair, was at a powerful apex with the then make-or-break *Pitchfork* review, engrossed with electroclash, the Strokes' leather jacket swagger and spiny electric guitars.[1] Phair's latest album didn't fit neatly in with any of that, and critics on all sides panned her for it.[2]

As is often the case, most of the negative reviews were by men, dismissive of music that specifically appealed to young women. Pitchfork notoriously gave it a 0.0 score, calling it "gratuitous and overdetermined" and full of "pointless f-bombs, manipulative ballads, and foul-mouthed shmeminism."[3] *The Guardian* said

---

1   Barshad, Amos. "When Critics Could Kill." *Slate*, May 1, 2018, https://slate.com/culture/2018/05/when-a-negative-pitchfork-review-could-end-a-career.html (accessed January 5, 2019).

2   "Liz Phair by Liz Phair." *Metacritic*, 24 June 2003, www.metacritic.com/music/liz-phair/liz-phair (accessed December 26, 2018)

3   Lemay, Matt. "Liz Phair - Liz Phair." *Pitchfork,* June 24, 2003, https://pitchfork.com/reviews/albums/6255-liz-phair (accessed December 15, 2018).

Phair was "crass and bloated, her lyrics crude and her image apparently a grotesque exercise in self-parody."[4] And the *New York Times* eulogized the album as "an embarrassing form of career suicide."[5] On top of it all, she was branded with a scarlet Sell Out letter for her vocal decision to make a commercial pop record (though she was hardly the first artist to do so).

In many ways, career suicide was precisely what the album ended up being. It produced two radio hits ("Why Can't I?" and "Extraordinary") and nearly matched her highest-selling album to date, but Phair's career withered in the aftermath. Her follow-up, 2005's *Somebody's Miracle*, sold less than a quarter of *Liz Phair*, and until recent reclamations and reexaminations of Phair's impact, her reputation never really recovered.[6]

Men can make mediocre art and withstand middling reviews from the *Pitchforks* of the world. They're allowed to make the "comeback" album and rarely have to mention the "bad" album again. Women cannot afford to make the same mistakes, cannot afford to produce anything that isn't perfect, lest it derail their careers indefinitely. It seems they are forever trapped by an expectation to repeatedly prove their talent to audiences that still sometimes view them as inferior or novelties.

A throughline in many reviews was *Exile in Guyville*, Phair's iconic 1993 debut. Unsurprising, as when we talk about Liz Phair,

---

4   Sweeting, Adam. "Liz Phair, Liz Phair." *The Guardian*, October 9, 2003, https://www.theguardian.com/music/2003/oct/10/popandrock9 (accessed December 15, 2018).

5   O'Rourke, Meghan. "Liz Phair's Exile in Avril-ville." *The New York Times*, June 22, 2003, https://www.nytimes.com/2003/06/22/arts/music-liz-phair-s-exile-in-avril-ville.html (accessed December 15, 2018).

6   Trust, Gary. "Ask Billboard: Kylie 'Fever.'" *Billboard*, July 16, 2010, https://www.billboard.com/articles/columns/chart-beat/957331/ask-billboard-kylie-fever (accessed December 26, 2018).

much of the conversation tends to focus on *Guyville*. And how could we not? Crafting a sharp, incisive, track-by-track response to the Rolling Stones' *Exile on Main Street* that bridged the gap between riot grrrl and indie rock is no small feat for a woman in her early twenties. But in the decades since its release, the album's critical success and stature have served more as a ball and chain, something all Phair's subsequent work would be unfairly measured against.

With *Liz Phair*, critics argued, Phair committed the ultimate betrayal: She didn't make *Exile in Guyville: Part Four*. In fact, she didn't even make an album that they could strictly categorize as rock. In music, it often seems as if the only thing worse than being a teen girl is making pop music that speaks to her— especially if you swerve from your rock lane to do so. Their reviews made false equivalences between the albums' tracks—the raunchy "HWC" wasn't as sly as "Flower"; "Why Can't I?" was *aw shucks* and saccharine where "Fuck and Run" was self-aware and casually explicit. The album as a whole was just too poppy, too youthful, too...not what they unjustly expected.

We say we want the artists we love and respect to evolve from album to album, but what we really mean is that we want them to do it our way, not theirs. We've made an investment in them, all those hours spent listening to their confessions, their expressive melodies that remain fresh no matter how many times we hit repeat. We feel like we know them, and, in a way, they help us know ourselves. There's comfort in the stability of beloved albums. No matter what happens in the ever-changing world around us, the record will always be the same, sound forever preserved in time. Sometimes we selfishly put unfair expectations on artists— neglecting to see them as humans, rather than album-making machines—to also stay the same for our own benefit.

This indignant expectation can best be seen in a 2003 *Spin* interview with Liz Phair and Chuck Klosterman, where the two disagree about Phair's album's pop intentions:[7]

PHAIR: That confessional stuff you liked so much—that was really just the sense of intimacy I was known for. I would practically bring you into my own bed. I was kind of like an actress who would let herself be ugly and unfiltered on screen. But now I'm more like a leading lady going through the motions with the right lighting. Is that a good analogy?

KLOSTERMAN: That's a perfect analogy. But I find that sentiment depressing.

PHAIR: Really? That bums me out. I know exactly what you're saying, and I understand entirely, but to hear you say it's *depressing* makes me kind of sad. I don't know why *you* should be depressed. Do you feel like you've lost someone who could make you feel that way?

KLOSTERMAN: No, that's not it. It just seems like you've made this decision to—

PHAIR: You keep saying this was my *decision*. It wasn't a decision. Those songs just aren't there anymore. I'll let you go through my demos and look for them if you want. I think this record is depressing to you because it makes you feel that you've lost part of your own childhood, and you realize you can't get that back. But I can't make a twenty-five-year-old's record at the age of thirty-six. For me, it boils down to this question: Do I want to *seem* authentic, or do I want to *feel* authentic? And I chose *feel*.

Questioning if pop music is authentic isn't new. It's a debate that rock critics resuscitate at least once a decade—punk versus

---

7   Klosterman, Chuck. "The Exile Factor." *Spin*, July 15, 2003, https://www.spin.com/2003/07/exile-factor/ (accessed December 15, 2018).

disco, radio star versus video star, and so on and so forth. Though the term "rockism" wouldn't appear until a year after *Liz Phair*'s release, the ideology that guitar rock (which is inherently white, straight, and male) is somehow more "pure" than spirited pop (typically feminine) was the driving reason why many gave the album failing reviews.[8] Rather than throw up our hands and concede that pop and rock aren't always comparable, that both can have moments of brilliance and banality, we insist that one must definitively hold more artistic value than the other.

Klosterman, along with other rockist critics and listeners at the time, overlooked the pop progression that led to *Liz Phair*. *Pitchfork* claimed that Phair's greatest asset was her "inability to write a perfect pop song," but that couldn't be further from the truth.[9] Phair wrote plenty of serviceable pop songs before 2003. It's just that, if she wasn't singing about being their blowjob queen, the bulk of men reviewing her albums didn't really care all too much to listen.

"I think it gathered a whole bunch of critics ready to take a shot, who hadn't really been following my career for a number of years," Phair told PopEntertainment in 2005, addressing the backlash. "Simply because it was sort of exciting, the difference between this indie-cred artist from *Guyville* and this pop incarnation of the same person. They didn't follow me through the steps, the progression that led to that. They just kind of jumped on and began to compare and contrast the two extremes."[10]

---

8 Sanneh, Kalefa. "The Rap Against Rockism." *The New York Times*, October 31, 2004, https://www.nytimes.com/2004/10/31/arts/music/the-rap-against-rockism.html (accessed December 27, 2018).

9 Lemay, Matt. "Liz Phair—Liz Phair."

10 Jacobs, Jay S. "Liz Phair: Exile From Indieville." *PopEntertainment*, November 7, 2005, http://www.popentertainment.com/lizphair.htm (accessed December 27, 2018).

Indeed, Phair's catalog exemplifies all the shady, gray, power pop area that lies within the extremes of radio pop and mainstream hard rock. "Why Can't I?" and "Extraordinary" were pilloried for being collaborative efforts with the Matrix—the production and writing team who, at the time, had garnered fame for working on Avril Lavigne's edgy-but-still-very-much-PG-rated debut album—but they didn't come out of nowhere. When listening to Phair's discography chronologically, *Liz Phair* appears as a logical endpoint to a career that had gotten progressively poppier album by album.

Phair's pop leanings reach back into her earliest rough recordings under the Girly-Sound moniker. Straightforward, melodic pop bursts through lo-fi, barebones arrangements on tracks like "Suckerfish," "Open Season," and the Knack-reminiscent "Gigolo." Throughout the tapes, Phair attempts, to the best of her and a four-track recorder's ability, to play up the pop sound, often manipulating or speeding up her vocals to sound younger and girlier.[11] The pop influence is there, too, on *Guyville*, though disguised by explicit lyrics that caught the most attention. Songs like "Never Said" and "Divorce Song" ring with wry lyrics on top of hooky choruses and hard-edged guitars while the lyrical candor of "Fuck and Run" distracts from its deceptively catchy, pop-radio friendly melody.

Phair continued to explore pop structures throughout *Whip-Smart* and *whitechocolatespaceegg*, both released in the mid- to late nineties, just before the boom of millennium pop. Both albums brim with euphoric, electrifying power pop jams. *Whip-Smart*'s "Supernova" and "May Queen" are giddy and rip-roaring, crackling and riff-filled, impossible not to roll your windows down and sing loudly along to. On *whitechocolatespaceegg*, "Polyester

---

11   Zaleski, Annie. "Liz Phair on 'Girly-Sound,' what guys don't get about 'Exile in Guyville' & what changed after Trump." *Salon*, May 5, 2018 (accessed December 18, 2018).

Bride" shines as the just-right balance of sugary melodicism, while "Baby Got Going" chugs with a kiss of rockabilly influence.

"You leave *Whip-Smart* wondering what a few dollops of actual production could add to Phair's levelheaded life chronicles," *Entertainment Weekly* wrote in their review of *Whip-Smart*.[12] Fulfilling that question, each album shows how much fuller Phair could make her music with the proper resources. Songs she first crafted as bareboned Girly-Sound demos reappear on both *Whip-Smart* and *whitechocolatespaceegg*, their arrangements tighter, the layers more lush, the mixes more polished. This power pop sensibility was always inside of her, always part of her work. The glossy production of *Liz Phair* makes sense as a next step.

At the same time, each album also seemed to test how much she could get away with. If *Guyville* was how much aggressive male ego she could strip away, each subsequent album became an opportunity to see just how much female ego she could assert. Once addressing male rock history was taken out of the equation, each album became more about asserting herself not as a female artist to be digested in comparison to men, but an artist to be listened to and respected in her own right.

At some point in their lifetimes, many women realize that to be agreeable is to be deceptive. Phair was acutely aware of the fine tightrope walk between who you really are versus who you are supposed to be. "Men would prefer to ignore women's complications," she told Rolling Stone in 1994, "because it's a natural instinct to ignore any complications that aren't your own."[13]

---

12   Browne, David. "Whip-Smart." *Entertainment Weekly*, September 24, 1994, https://ew.com/article/1994/09/23/whip-smart/ (accessed January 5, 2019).

13   Dunn, Jancee. "Q&A: Liz Phair." *Rolling Stone*, January 27, 1994, https://www.rollingstone.com/music/music-news/qa-liz-phair-230688/ (accessed December 15, 2018).

To pair two strongly feminine qualities together—a glossy pop production with confessional, "girly" lyrics—is to invite ridicule at best, ostracization at worst. If Phair wanted to play with the guys, but still tell Guyville to fuck off on behalf of all girls, she could be a Trojan horse in the scene. She could disguise personal, complicated, and female lyrics in rough rock arrangements, occasionally letting pop sentiment sneak in, almost like a wink to the girls that she was still with them. But, it's as if, after growing older and experiencing marriage, motherhood, and divorce in the ten years between *Guyville* and *Liz Phair*, she had outgrown it all. She didn't want to be the tongue-in-cheek blowjob queen anymore; her lyrics shifted toward topics that were appropriate for where she was in her life—more whole, more complicated, more mature. If that was cold water on the male libido, so be it.

Done with playing the unwinnable game, she leaned harder into a pop sound so many disdained—because she liked it, because it was what she wanted to do, and, because, perhaps most of all, it was what sold. If people were really paying attention, they could have seen this coming. After all, Phair proclaimed her belief that "it's nice to be liked, but better by far to get paid" on *whitechocolatespaceegg*'s "Shitloads of Money." Who cared if they hated the album? She didn't have to win critics' affection, but she could get paid.

The truth is, reducing *Liz Phair* to being a "bad" album by simply not living up to the impossibly high standard set by *Exile in Guyville* hardly holds any weight as criticism. It was just a lazy comparison that bounced around the echo chamber of rock criticism and stuck.

Phair said it best in 2005: "If you are an old fan, and it doesn't fit what you need, don't buy the disc."[14] Fifteen years later, Phair is

---

14   Carr, David. "The Independence of Liz Phair." *The New York Times*, August 2, 2005, https://www.nytimes.com/2005/08/02/arts/music/the-independence-of-liz-phair.html (accessed December 15, 2018).

making a comeback, and the same men who not only refused to buy the disc but abandoned her en masse in the early aughts are now crowding the stage, blocking the views of the young women who wanted to be there all along.

That's the thing about Liz Phair's discography. A pop thread runs through it, but there's something for everyone. If you don't like one album, you don't have to abandon her for good—I don't expect *Liz Phair* and *Exile in Guyville* to elicit the same feelings when I listen to them. Each album fulfills a different craving for the listener, much as it fulfills a different creative desire from an artist. After all, getting trapped in a cycle of constantly listening to or creating the same *thing* repeatedly doesn't mean the *thing* is good; it means the *thing* is safe. And safe is one thing Liz Phair will never be.

Carrie Courogen *is a New York-based culture writer and social editor at* Condé Nast. *Her writing—which often focuses on the intersection of feminism and pop culture—has been published by* NPR, Pitchfork, Vice, PAPER Magazine, Guitar World, Flood Magazine, *and the* New York Daily News, *among others. Since 2017, she has coproduced '77 Music Club, a podcast dedicated to examining albums of decades past through the lens of today.*

Never Got to Say Goodbye:
The Power of Pop

By Joe Clifford

T HEY SAY NEVER MEET your heroes. I think they mean that because heroes are bound to disappoint you. I'm pretty sure it's the other way around. How the hell do you tell another grown man he's changed your life? That a decision he made to rejoin a band translated into reconciliation with your dying brother? That a song he helped write yielded a letter from beyond the grave? You can't. Not without sounding like a fucking moron.

When I set out to interview Franz Nicolay, recently reinstated multi-instrumentalist/keyboardist for the Hold Steady, I was woefully unprepared. Oh, I had my questions. I'd done my research. Most of all, I'd been an unabashed advocate of the band from the beginning—hardcore, scars and war, never-miss-a-show fan. Man, fan doesn't come close. Raised on Springsteen, only three bands matter to me in a post-Bruce-inspired world: Frank Turner, the Gaslight Anthem, and the Hold Steady. As an author, I cite lyricists as my greatest literary influences.

"If you're talking about the difference between long-form prose and writing lyrics for pop songs," Franz says, "[L]ong-form prose forces you to be more specific."

The assignment was simple: ask Franz a few questions about what he thought of power pop and create a narrative arc that shows how the band fits into the genre.

Fine. I'd ask a couple perfunctory questions about power pop, get the ball rolling, and then get into the cool shit I was really interested in, like why Franz decided to come back ("So people would stop asking me if I was rejoining the band") and what was next for the Hold Steady ("[If you know I can't answer this] then why are you asking me?"), and then we'd bond, maybe get some coffee, and now that he lives down the street, we'd become best friends.

My entire approach was fucked.

I started with a softball, asking Franz if he considers the Hold Steady power pop. I assumed he'd bristle at the term, which, to some, has come to encapsulate bands like Blink-182 and Sum 41, and even though I can admit to liking those bands, Franz can reassemble an accordion from scratch, is classically trained; he's not running down the street naked, brat-screeching about prank calls and sodomy. I'd come back with bands like Big Star, Cheap Trick, and he'd come around to my way of thinking. But he didn't bristle. Instead he asked me how I'd define the term.

And I realized I personally have no fucking idea. Like art, I know it when I see it. Or in this case, hear it. Pressed, panicked, put on the spot, I gave some bullshit answer, something about driving sixteenth notes, crunching, distorted guitars, and "poppy" beats, which is tantamount to answering a high school essay about the Peloponnesian War by stating it's about "a war in Peloponnesia" (I know it's actually "Peloponnese." But the fact that I only know that because I had to Google that shit just proves my point). It's a term most easily defined by what it's not. It's not R&B, it's not hip-hop, classic rock, soul, etc.

"It's morphed into pop punk," Franz says. "Pop punk is what people under forty would call power pop...I always think of bands like Big Star and the Replacements as 'rock critic' bands...bands that are critically unassailable."

Like irony, I realized the term has both a literal and interpretive connotation. Literal? You can use Google same as I can. The real question is what does *power pop* mean to me? Why do the Hold Steady, *for me*, fit so neatly in that niche? Here's what I've come up with.

Some nights the painkillers make the pain even worse.

That is a Hold Steady line. And if the fucking Shins play it, it's not power pop. Pink Floyd, as great a lyricist as Roger Waters is, can't pull off that line. Cheap Trick can. Paul Westerberg can. Bruno Mars can't. Why? Because power pop is an ideal distilled, a blend of angst, ennui, and hope. It's balance, man. The line resonates most when you got a black and tan, tapping feet, cigarette hanging from lips, and four pills you aren't sure whether you should take. Because you care about that girl, maybe even love her even if she doesn't love herself, but you're watching her sell herself short by going off with that asshole and watching her kill herself is killing you. But he's the one holding her tonight, and all you have are these feelings you can't get out. You're either one of us. Or you're not. And if you get that, then thanks for listening, thanks for understanding, and we're that much closer because of it.

The Hold Steady was the soundtrack of my grad school years, 2006 being the year *Boys and Girls in America* came out. It's the record many consider the band's masterpiece. I've always liked the follow-ups to perceived masterpieces. I'll take *Darkness on the Edge of Town* over *Born to Run*, and I prefer *Stay Positive* to *Boys and Girls*. But that's quibbling. All are fantastic albums. The Hold

Steady played on continuous loop when my drug-addict brother, Josh, came to Miami to help me convalesce following a near-fatal motorcycle accident that same year. His carrying my bent and broken body into the bathtub to help me shower might be the last happy memory I have of him.

Grad school almost killed me. But it's where I learned how to write by learning I was nothing special, that I was mortal, could break, and could die. By learning I was nothing special, I finally understood that I had to start working harder, smarter, accept that talent alone only gets you through the door. While in Florida, I was fortunate to study under some of the best mystery writers in the country. Working so hard to become a writer, I alienated my young (second) wife. I got divorced. I got that motorcycle. I ended up on the pavement, gushing blood. I won't call it a lesson. Because, like Craig Finn says, life isn't a romantic comedy; in the end no one learns a lesson.

"The stakes are different," Franz says. "We're [probably] not gonna get bigger than we are right now. But there's an audience of people who really care about it."

I'm not kidding when I say the Hold Steady changed my life. Yeah, shit like that gets thrown around. Music that is life changing. I think of Natalie Portman in *Garden State* telling Zach Braff the Shins would change his life. I like the movie, I love Natalie Portman, and I think *Scrubs* is the greatest sitcom in the history of the world. But if the Shins are changing your life, your life's gotta suck.

Following grad school, I moved three thousand miles to get away from my brother and returned to San Francisco, the city that saw the start of my heroin addiction, because it was a helluva lot safer than returning to my home state of Connecticut with Josh. After that move is when my life started clicking into place. My books started getting published, money came in, a little notoriety. I got remarried. In fact, socially awkward as I was (am), I might never have asked out my neighbor, Justine, who eventually became the mother of my two kids, if I didn't have the Hold Steady as an excuse. I needed a date to the Fillmore. That's a lie. I would've gone alone. Just like I flew three thousand miles, alone, to see the Hold Steady at the Brooklyn Bowl for Massive Nights III this past November 2018.

Massive Nights, culled from an HS lyric, is a yearly event, held ever since Franz came back, an event, sadly, I'd missed the last two years.

When I first heard Franz was rejoining the band, I was working on a book around midnight. I let out a Howard Dean whoop from my desk, waking up my wife and kids. I immediately called my brother, who never slept, and told him we had to go see them. Who knew how long Franz was sticking around? How many more shows the band was going to play?

I'm not saying the Hold Steady stopped producing great music when Franz left in 2010. But it wasn't the same. As good as *Heaven Is Whenever* and *Teeth Dreams* are, the Hold Steady isn't the same band without Franz. He is, as Rick Neilson once described Robin Zander, the secret weapon of the band.

I missed the first Massive Nights, 2016, because I was in Tahoe filming a book trailer for my latest Jay Porter novel, wishing I'd have known sooner so I could fly back east and bring my brother to the show. By that point, Josh and I were so far apart; the only thing we had left in common was baseball and rock and roll. The second year, 2017, I didn't get to go with my brother because he was dead.

When I finally made Massive Nights III, the trip was a pilgrimage. I was slated to leave for Italy on a book tour, and my wife (number three if anyone is keeping track) already wasn't happy. I was about to leave her with two young, wild boys to tour Europe for a month, but first I was going to fly three thousand miles for a couple of nights of rock shows in a bar? I saw her point. But I was going anyway.

It's hard to explain the need for music at this stage in my life. Maybe it's a mid-life crisis. Instead of screwing my students in the back of sports cars, I returned to the sport of my youth (golf) and started catching more rock shows. We all need to stay young somehow. In the afterword to the second ed. of *Junkie Love*, I wrote how my brother always bet the fifth horse in the sixth race. Which is true. My brother, in addition to being a raging alcoholic and drug addict, also had a bad gambling problem. To my knowledge, that horse was never named Chips Ahoy, and it never came in. But rock and roll is a pretty strong surrogate when you can't talk to someone; and it makes a pretty good replacement drug when they take away the good stuff. It's why we cobble mixed tapes for the girls we like. We need someone else to talk for us in our most tender moments.

"When things are going badly and you're on your own," Franz says, "You can sort of take this masochist pleasure in it. But if there are other people implicated, then it feels like being selfish."

For the last ten years of my brother's life, I was only able to communicate with Josh two ways. The first was the Jay Porter books I wrote, the alienated story of addicted brothers. The second, the CDs I'd burn. Forget mp3s, my brother only wanted CDs. (I'd try to give him an iPod later, which he'd sell for drugs. He was not, as Bad Religion says, a "21st Century Digital Boy.") Every time I came back east, he wanted new music. Frank. Fallon. And the Hold Steady. They did my talking for me.

The last time I saw my brother, we were in Boston, where my sister lives. I know my brother loved me. And he knew I loved him. But the distance between men can be unbridgeable at times. He thought I was a dick. I thought he was a dick. That was our go-to line: "You're a dick." Only later did I realize, like a perverted *Princess Bride*, it was our twisted way of saying I love you.

That afternoon in Boston, Josh, my baby brother by four years, the little boy I taught to throw a baseball, looked twenty years older than me. His hair had gone white, and his skin was stained mustard yellow by the jaundice. We went bowling. I have some pictures from that day. I look at them a lot. Me, my brother, my two sons, also four years apart. For the most part, I held it together.

There was one moment, though, at the very end where it started getting to me.

So I go to sit outside. It's cold. The early onset of winter, October in Boston. I'm freezing my ass off. I'm basically watching my little brother kill himself, and there's nothing I can do about it. He comes outside and sits next to me. No one says anything. Then he throws one of his big arms around me (my brother was huge, 6'5", 300+), and hugs me. It was an odd display of tenderness coming from him. The air was so cold it made my eyes water.

My timeline is probably fucked up. But the way I recall it, a month later he was dead. Then the Hold Steady released its first new track with Franz (and third guitarist Steve Selvidge), "The Entitlement Crew."

> *Your brother's in Boston*
> *He's acting like a dick*
> *I remember back before*
> *We knew he was sick*
> *Thanks for listening*
> *Thanks for understanding*

Can't you see how I feel I've been abandoned?
Never got to say goodbye to you...

Now obviously Craig Finn, Franz Nicolay, and co. don't give a shit about my strained relationship with my brother, and that line was certainly not written with us in mind. But that is the power of pop, the perfect dysfunctional marriage of words and music. The song isn't a ballad, and it's not some auto-tuned, mass-produced pap made palatable to the unwashed masses. "The Entitlement Crew" is the best track the Hold Steady has released since "Stay Positive." It's driven by Tad and Steve's palm-muted, distorted guitars and Bobby and Galen's lock-step backbeat, but the glue is Franz's keys, which are back, front and center, for the first time in ten years. In between Craig's painfully familiar story about a party that goes on too long and costs too much, it's the *Boys and Girls* synth and piano that buoy the lyrics and make them ring, sting.

And this is how a resurrection *really* feels. Because it reminds me that, even after all the shit I've been through, the hits and losses, the knockdowns and staggering to my feet, I still have a heart that can break. And that's a good goddamn thing.

After Josh died and I delivered the eulogy, half the fucking church blaming me because I was the one who got him started on the drugs, which isn't entirely true—Josh was already drinking heavily in middle school—but, yeah, sure, I didn't help, I sat in my rented car and blasted "Entitlement Crew." I'm not saying sitting outside St. Paul's Church in my hometown, my brother on his way to the box, was a religious experience. But listening to that song and those lines made me feel a fuck lot better.

"The abstraction you're allowed in [pop songs]," Franz says, "you can throw a line in just because it sounds cool."

In the summer of 2018, I caught all three Hold Steady shows in San Francisco. I drank J&B scotch for the first time in almost thirty years. The first time I ever drank—never mind got drunk; the first time I *tasted* hard alcohol—was when I downed an entire bottle of J&B after Sherry Gagliardi rejected me, or maybe it was Katie Ross or Amy Krois. I can't remember. There were a lot of girls I was in love with in college. And a lot of drugs in between those years. But some dude passed me a bottle toward the end of show at the Rickshaw, and I figured if I'm ever going to drink J&B again, this is the time.

A few months later, I flew out to see the band in New York for Massive Nights III. At the last minute, I got ahold of our cousin, Jason, who lives in the city, and he joined me for one of the shows. I broke a bunch of bones in that bad motorcycle accident in grad school. I think I've mentioned it before. Makes it hard to stand for long, almost impossible to dance. But it's not like I could dance before the accident. I can do what all middle-aged white guys do at concerts. Get as close as I can and jump and sing along and pretend I'm young again, that my whole life is still ahead of me, that I won't make the same mistakes and let down the people I love. So I patched up with Lidocaine, took all the pain meds I'm allowed to by law, ditched the cane, and got as close to the stage as I could. I raised a toast to St. Joe Strummer and sang along to all those sing-a-long songs. It was a religious experience.

I'm not religious, and I sure as fuck ain't spiritual. But I believe in God. If I had to define my faith, I'd say I'm a Springsteen Catholic: I believe in the love that you gave me; I believe in the faith that can save me.

Maybe it was the beer. Maybe it was the church of rock and roll. Maybe it was the conversations I still have with my dead brother, where he talks to me, only now we say the things to each other we never could when he was alive; and his voice is as loud and clear as if he were standing in this same room beside me. Those shows touched me, made me feel whole again, if not forgiven.

I can't rewrite wasted lives, and I can't fix all the shit I got wrong. But I'll take these annual reminders, because we can all be something bigger.

Damn right, you'll rise again.

Joe Clifford *is the author of several books, including* The One That Got Away, Junkie Love, *and the* Jay Porter Thriller Series, *as well as editor of the anthologies* Trouble in the Heartland: Crime Fiction Inspired by the Songs of Bruce Springsteen; Just to Watch Them Die: Crime Fiction Inspired by the Songs of Johnny Cash; *and* Hard Sentences, *which he coedited. Joe's writing can be found at www.joeclifford.com.*

My So-Called (Power Pop) Life

By David Bash

M Y LOVE OF POWER pop dates back to May 1972, when an unknown band called the Raspberries paid a visit to my junior high school and put on a show for us. I remember some of it well: we went to the auditorium and saw a white piano and a bunch of guitars, and then four guys in white suits came out, one of whom yelled, "Hey, you wanna hear a dirty song?" And of course all of us prepubescents responded with a lusty "yeah!"

What followed was a sound like I had never heard before. Those chord changes, the power, that Beatles-on-steroids melody; it was absolutely amazing. Of course the song was "Go All The Way," and although I'd never heard the phrase "power pop," this moment began a lifelong love affair with the sub-genre.

I'd been listening to Top 40 music for a couple of years and essentially loved all of it, but kinda "outgrew" it by the mid-seventies when album rock started to take over. A few years later, power pop took root on both Top 40 stations and heavier FM radio. Unlike most fans of power pop, I didn't see the power pop revolution as a "refreshing change," but rather as a welcome augmentation; it was great to hear bands like Cheap Trick, Shoes, the Rubinoos, Off Broadway, and so many others grace the radio waves, and, man, did I want more of it.

When I began collecting records in the mid-seventies, I was voracious and also very much a "risk taker" in that if I saw an album that "looked right," I would take a chance and buy it. With power pop, there seemed to be a lot of covers featuring four kinda wimpy-looking guys with medium length hair holding guitars and smiling, and song titles with a lot of girls' names in them. That's how I found a lot of my power pop until I began reading *Goldmine Magazine* in the early eighties, and first saw ads for obscure power pop like the Toms' glorious album and an unknown gem called *Beauty and Sadness* by some band called the Smithereens. Soon after, when "college rock" emerged, I began frequenting a record shop in Encinitas, California, called Off The Record. The store's manager, Phil Galloway, learned my taste pretty quickly, turning me on to all kinds of power pop, especially bands from the UK and Australia like the Direct Hits and Ups and Downs, to name a few.

My power pop love and expertise continued to grow, but for several years I thought I was a lone wolf; occasionally I'd see some guy in a record shop holding cool power pop albums, but my conversations with them would invariably lead nowhere. All of this ended with the appearance of *Yellow Pills* magazine, which I stumbled on one day at Off The Record. In it were reviews of all kinds of power pop discs I'd never heard of (along with several, yikes, cassettes!), and the publisher/editor, Jordan Oakes, seemed like a really cool guy who knew his shit. Based on the letters he would print in the issues, it became clear to me that there was an audience out there who specifically loved power pop. Remember, this is before that wonderful albatross known as the internet, so there were very few avenues to find like-minded people.

Soon afterward I became acquainted with John Borack, another like mind who had been writing about power pop in *Goldmine Magazine* for several years. Still, I was pretty arrogant, thinking I knew more about power pop than anyone else, so when I met John I went in like a lion...and came out a lamb. John turned me on to so many bands, like the Gravelberrys, the Cheepskates, and Racer X (but I made up for it by turning him on to an equal number of obscure sixties bands).

I wanted to do what Jordan and John did. Luckily, this dovetailed nicely with the oncoming "power pop renaissance" taking place in the mid-nineties, when magazines covering power pop started springing up from all over. Within a year, I was writing reviews for *Yellow Pills*, its new competitors *Audities*, *Amplifier*, and *Pop Sided*, and *Goldmine Magazine*'s biggest rival, *Discoveries*. It was so much fun, and when word got around about what I was doing, I came to discover and love that golden ticket known as the "promo." My so-called power pop life was really good, and about to get even better.

In January of 1995 I moved to the LA area and lived in West Hills. I soon found out about the flourishing pop scene in Los Angeles, and I was absolutely floored by the amount of talent. I discovered bands like the Negro Problem, the Andersons, the Sugarplastic (great to see so many bands with "The" in their name, after all the grunge bands saw "the" as anathema), Baby Lemonade, and so many others. What's more, when I went to see these bands play, I saw members of other bands in the crowd, cheering them on. This was my first exposure to anything resembling a "scene," and I took it all in voraciously, getting to know the band members personally and writing reviews of their CDs.

The man most responsible for this scene was Tony Perkins, who had been putting on bi-weekly shows called "Bubblegum Crisis" for more than a year, which featured pop and punk bands from LA, and had been doing a wonderful job showcasing them. Perkins also had a fine band of his own, the cheekily named

Martin Luther Lennon. In 1996, Perkins put together a music festival called Poptopia that featured most of the pop bands from LA, along with a few out-of-towners for flavor. It was like a circus of pop, and it attracted people from all over the world, and I would become friends with many. I was in heaven, but I was also envious of the attention Perkins was getting, a feeling I filed away in the recesses of my brain, which would emerge in the not too distant future...but more on that later.

What was becoming very clear to me was that there was a burgeoning power pop scene all over the world. Bands would contact me from everywhere, asking me to review their CDs. At the same time, a gentleman named Bruce Brodeen was forming a label/mail order company called Not Lame Records, which released and/or carried all kinds of power pop CDs. Bruce and I formed a bond that lasts to this day.

In the meantime, the Los Angeles scene was becoming even stronger. There was a lot of hope in the city, as some of the bands were being signed to David Geffen's "baby band" label, DreamWorks. That, coupled with the Silverlake scene and the "Dust Brothers" group of bands, there was the thought that Los Angeles could become "the new Seattle."

Meanwhile, many bands from outside of LA asked me for info about Poptopia. So when Tony Perkins was booking the 1997 festival, I asked him if I could help funnel bands his way. He agreed, and I sent several, but as Poptopia was first and foremost an "LA festival," he didn't have a lot of room for bands from elsewhere. Those that didn't make the bill would commiserate with me, lamenting about not being accepted into the festival. Suddenly, a light came on...

Near the end of 1997 I was having lunch with my friend, music attorney Ben McLane, and told him about the many bands who wanted to come to Los Angeles to play their music. I had been thinking about Poptopia and had convinced myself that I could do something similar. I relayed this to Ben, saying, "I'd like to do my own music festival, with more of an emphasis on galvanizing a worldwide pop scene under one roof." He agreed, which was all the encouragement I needed. So one night when a very cool pop show was happening at Jack's Sugar Shack, which I knew most of the LA pop scene would be attending, I announced my intentions. The responses were mostly positive, but over the next few months I heard from several people who said, "I'm not sure this is going to work; will people come out to see a bunch of bands from outside Los Angeles that they've never heard of?" This made some sense, but I was determined to do the festival anyway and had no intention of compromising my vision.

In the meantime, I needed a name for the festival; one day I was speaking to my friend, Brian Kassan (main man of another great LA band, Chewy Marble). I told him I wanted something to emphasize an international pop scene converging under one roof, and he replied "hmm…international…pop…" And then it hit me: International Pop Overthrow!

The name emphasized two things: 1) A worldwide pop scene getting together in order to "overthrow" mainstream radio, which was sucking pretty hard around that time; 2) Tribute paid to the band Material Issue, whose debut album was called *International Pop Overthrow* (their primary songwriter and lead vocalist, Jim Ellison, had tragically taken his own life not long before, and I felt it was right to honor him in this way).

I could write a book about International Pop Overthrow, and perhaps someday I will, but for now I'm proud to say that the naysayers were absolutely wrong about the success of the festival. Our first event took place in August of 1998, in LA and nearby

Orange County, and it was a rousing success. Since then we've branched out into several other cities throughout the US and Canada, along with Stockholm, Sweden, and our most special place, Liverpool, UK, with all shows being held at the World Famous Cavern Club (yes, that one).

I should point out that, without Poptopia, there would never have been an International Pop Overthrow. I used Tony Perkins' model as a launching off point for IPO, and while I've adjusted several things over the years, I owe Tony a great deal of gratitude for showing me the way.

This year marks the twenty-second IPO Los Angeles, and although there hasn't been a "pop scene" in LA for several years, you can bet we'll be featuring a lot of awesome local bands, along with others from all over the place. Our hope is that as long as IPO exists, the power pop light will shine brightly throughout the world.

David Bash *is the Founder/CEO of the International Pop Overthrow Music Festival (www.internationalpopoverthrow.com), which is held annually in various cities throughout the US and Canada, as well as in Liverpool (at The World Famous Cavern Club!) and Stockholm. He is also a pop music journalist who writes for* Shindig! *and* Ugly Things *magazines, and rockandrollglobe. com, and is one of the Executive Producers of* The Power Pop Movie, *slated for release in early 2020. He's written liner notes for several CDs, and has a music collection the size of Mt. Rushmore. Bash lives with his wife, Rina Bardfield, and their cat Ombre, in Reseda, California.*